ARCHITECTURAL

HERITAGE V

ARCHITECTURAL

*The Journal of
the Architectural Heritage Society of Scotland*

HERITAGE V

EDINBURGH

University Press

The Architectural Heritage Society of Scotland

Glasite Meeting House
33 Barony Street
Edinburgh EH6 6NX
Tel: (0131) 557 0019

Manuscripts for submission to *Architectural Heritage* should be sent to John Lowrey, c/o the Architectural Heritage Society of Scotland, as above.

Architectural Heritage V is the twenty-first issue of the *Journal of the Architectural Heritage Society of Scotland* (formerly the *Scottish Georgian Society*). Backnumbers (1, 7–11, 13 and 15) are available from the Society. *Architectural Heritage I: William Adam* (1990), *Architectural Heritage II: Scottish Architects Abroad* (1991), *Architectural Heritage III: The Age of Mackintosh* (1992) and *Architectural Heritage IV: Robert Adam* are available directly from Edinburgh University Press.

Membership of the Society entitles members to receive both *Architectural Heritage* and the regular *Newsletters* free of charge. The Society exists to promote the protection and study of Scotland's historic architecture. Details of membership can be obtained from the Society's headquarters.

© The Architectural Heritage Society
of Scotland, 1995 (1994 issue)

Edinburgh University Press Ltd
22 George Square, Edinburgh

Typeset in Monotype Perpetua
by Nene Phototypesetters Ltd,
Northampton, and printed and
bound in Great Britain

A CIP record of this book
is available from the
British Library

ISBN 0 7486 0706 4

CONTENTS

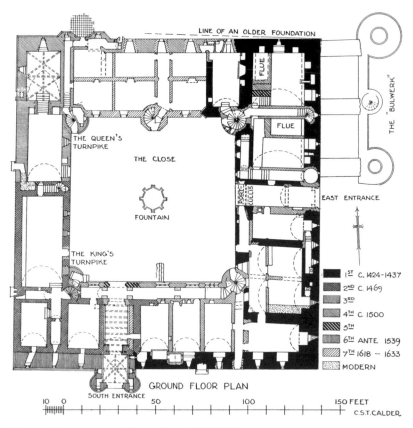

LINE OF AN OLDER FOUNDATION

FLUE

FLUE

THE QUEEN'S
TURNPIKE

THE CLOSE

THE "BULWERK"

FOUNTAIN

THE KING'S
TURNPIKE

EAST ENTRANCE

1ST C. 1424-1437
2ND C. 1469
3RD
4TH C. 1500
5TH
6TH ANTE 1539
7TH 1618 – 1633
MODERN

GROUND FLOOR PLAN

SOUTH ENTRANCE

10 0   50   100   150 FEET
                                                      C.S.T.CALDER

1.1 Linlithgow Palace, 1425 and later, plans. (RCAHMS)

1.2 Linlithgow Palace, 1425 and later, aerial view. (John Dewar)

IAN CAMPBELL

Linlithgow's 'Princely Palace' and its Influence in Europe

James III and James IV transformed James I's French-inspired palace into a Scoto-Italian palazzo, unparalled in northern Europe, and, hence, worthy of imitation in some of the most significant buildings in sixteenth- and early seventeenth-century France, Denmark and Germany.

MARY OF GUISE, James V's second queen, on first setting eyes on Linlithgow Palace in 1538, is reported to have said that she had never seen a more princely palace. Such unqualified praise from someone brought up at the court of François I seems so unlikely, that her remark is usually paraphrased to the effect that Linlithgow Palace compared well with the châteaux of France.[1] The present article will seek to demonstrate that Mary's words can be taken at face value. Firstly, it will show how by the reign of James IV (1488–1513), Linlithgow was probably the most advanced Renaissance palace north of the Alps, rather than accepting the conventional view that the Renaissance arrived with Mary of Guise.[2] It will then go on to suggest that Linlithgow Palace was admired enough to appear to have been imitated from France to Denmark.

The earliest parts of the present palace were erected by James I (1406–37), after he was released from English captivity in 1424. Between 1425 and his death, James built what is now the east range, or quarter, and adjacent parts of the north and south quarters, making a C-shaped plan (Figure 1.1). From 1429, records refer to it as a 'palace', the first documented purpose-built by a Scots king.[3]

James III (1460–88) continued the south quarter ending it in a quadrangular corner tower, and began the southern part of the west quarter, probably already with the intention of creating an enclosed courtyard.[4] James IV achieved this aim, building the north west tower and remodelling much of the earlier parts, including James I's great hall, the 'Lyon Chalmer', and adding towers to the north-east and south-east corners. He also built the 'Bulwark', a forework on the east front.[5] The palace seems to have been virtually complete by the time of James IV's death at the battle of Flodden in 1513, but, in the mid-1530s, James V (1513–42) created a new main entrance in the south-west corner, preceded by a small free-standing gateway, decorated with open bartisans and the insignia of the four orders of chivalry to which he belonged. He also undertook a few finishing touches and some limited remodelling in areas such as the Lyon Chalmer and the chapel.[6] The present north range was constructed in 1618–24 for James VI, following the collapse of the original in 1607. The palace then remained largely unaltered until 1746 when it was burnt out and left unroofed.[7]

Thus, by the reign of James IV, Linlithgow Palace had assumed the broad lines of its present appearance, i.e. a quadrangular enclosed courtyard, with four turnpike stairs, projecting into the corners of the court, and four gabled towers, remarkable for its symmetry and general regularity of planning (Figure 1.2).[8] The external façades were all marked by battlements and the virtual absence of windows near ground level, suggesting that security was not taken for granted, although it was clearly never intended to withstand a concerted attack.[9] Some have accordingly typified it as a fortified manor house, and looked to fourteenth-century northern English examples of quadrilateral castles with corner towers, such as Lumley in County Durham, as sources of the design.[10]

James I may have seen Lumley in March 1424, during the negotiations in Durham for his release from imprisonment.[11] However, if he did, he clearly did not feel moved to imitate it at Linlithgow, since his new palace was neither quadrangular, nor had towers. Rather his masons seem to have been looking to France for inspiration and the similarity has been noted between Linlithgow and early fifteenth-century French châteaux such as Pierrefonds and La Ferté-Milon.[12] Linlithgow also resembles La Ferté-Milon in its continuous machicolated parapet and lack of protruding towers. The French chatêaux were built around 1400 by Louis, duke of Orleans, and James I could have known of them from Louis' son, Charles, who shared his captivity in England from 1415, or from some of the 6,000 Scots, who went to fight for the French in 1419. He may even have seen them for himself while on campaign with the English army in 1420–1.[13]

If James I was not impressed by northern English fortified manor houses, it is even less likely that James III and James IV were, given that their ambitions and tastes were so progressive in other spheres, and that in other areas of Scottish architecture, English influence was being rejected.[14] Virtually the only English-looking feature of Linlithgow is the elevation of the 'transe', the three-storied gallery or corridor with, square-headed, three- and four-light mullioned windows, added on to the courtyard side of the south quarter, probably balancing one on the north quarter. Some attribute its appearance to English masons, following in the wake of James IV's marriage to Margaret Tudor, Henry VII of England's daughter, in 1503, but firm evidence is lacking.[15] The use of galleries, however, had been an established feature of Scottish royal palaces from at least 1461 in the east quarter at Falkland, following French or, more probably, Flemish fashion, since the palace belonged to James II's queen, Mary of Guelders, niece of Philip the Good, duke of Burgundy.[16] Thus, English influence at Linlithgow is at most minimal.

Others have suggested France as the source of inspiration for James III and James IV's additions, including Sir David Lindsay of the Mount in 1530, i.e. before James V's works.[17] French châteaux were becoming more regular in planning in the late fifteenth and early sixteenth centuries, and there are French mottoes carved on bosses in the king's private apartments in the north-west tower of Linlithgow, built by James IV.[18] Moreover, the turnpike stairs in the four corners of the courtyard, also built during his reign, certainly resemble

French examples. However, the most prominent new châteaux, such as Le Plessis-Bourrée, all follow the precedent of the late medieval Louvre and have circular projecting corner pavilions, until well into the sixteenth century, and hence cannot be considered as models for Linlithgow.[19]

The country with the closest parallels to Linlithgow is Italy, in particular the palace designs of Filarete and the Palazzo Venezia. By 1400 the quadrilateral fortress-palace with square corner towers had become standard in north Italy, following the example of prototypes such as the Castello Visconteo at Pavia (c. 1360–5), one of the most symmetrical and least fortress-like in appearance.[20] The type, sometimes known as the 'palacium ad modum castri', proved popular throughout the fifteenth and sixteenth centuries for signorial palaces both in town and country. The trappings of a castle unequivocally proclaiming to all the status of the occupants, by looking back to the age of chivalry, could be combined with the regularity of planning and application of *all'antica* detailing to apertures or surface treatment, which signalled to *cognoscenti* the patron's advanced Renaissance tastes.[21] In Filarete's treatise, written c. 1460 for the duke of Milan, the designs for the gentleman's and the duke's palaces are quadrangular with four square corner towers, the latter with an additional tower over the main entrance, while the bishop's palace with two corner towers on the front is conspicuous for its blind ground floor, all features which are paralled at Linlithgow.[22]

For the bishop's palace, Filarete probably had in mind the Palazzo Venezia in Rome. Shortly after his election in 1464, Pope Paul II began building a vast new palace.[23] Only two wings were finished as Paul intended but it appears a complete quadrangle was envisaged. The principal façade had a blind ground floor, a first floor with round-headed windows, large square-headed windows to the second floor, the *piano nobile*, and small square-headed windows to the third floor (Figure 1.3). Around the eaves run machicolations and crenellations, and from the south-east corner rises a quadrangular tower. Even incomplete, the Palazzo Venezia remains the most monumental quattrocento expression of the *palatium ad modum castri* in Italy, being described in 1471, by Borso d'Este, duke of Ferrara, as 'this most superb pontifical palace, exceeding in construction, in site, in magnificence, many many other royal palaces'.[24]

By making James I's palace quadrangular and adding square corner towers, James III and IV effectively made it an example of the *palatium ad modum castri*. This cannot have been forced on them by the constraints of the existing building, since James III's tower in the south-west corner was part of an extension beyond James I's palace. James IV may have decided to make the new north-west tower match his father's for reasons of symmetry, but, at the front it would have been simple enough to add circular pavilions at the two corners, following French fashion, rather than raising towers from the parapet as at the Palazzo Venezia.[25] In addition, the six identical square-headed windows on the east façade lighting the Lyon Chalmer, striking for their size, proportions of 2:1 height to width, and regularity of placing, can be compared with those of the *piano nobile* of the Palazzo Venezia

1.3 Palazzio Verezia, Rome, 1464 and later, east front.

1.4 Linlithgow Palace, 1425 and later, east front. (RCAHMS)

(Figure 1.4). Their outward splays suggest enlargement, which may have occurred when all the windows of the great hall were glazed and had new ironwork in 1511–12.[26]

The Renaissance character of the round-headed windows lighting the west side of the hall, overlooking the courtyard with their broad cavetto mouldings, has been recognised by others, who have consequently dated them to the 1530s. However, the accounts suggest that, although some work was done to them then, it was less than in 1511–12.[27] Also, they closely resemble those in the northern part of the west quarter, built by James IV, as testified by the ciphers on the corbels at the top of the turnpike in the north-west corner, bearing his initials and those of Margaret Tudor.[28] The Roman lettering of these ciphers is very similar to that on the brackets of the great hall at Edinburgh Castle, again demonstrating knowledge of Italian models.[29] The round-headed windows too probably derive from Italy, since they pre-date the earliest examples in France in the François I wing at Blois, begun only in 1515.[30] Round-headed windows are common in early Renaissance architecture throughout Italy, but the broad cavetto moulding is characteristic of the apertures of some Florentine palaces, such as the portals of the Medici and Strozzi palaces.

One feature at Linlithgow, the Renaissance character of which has hitherto been overlooked, is the great triple fireplace in the Lyon Chalmer with its lintel strongly reminiscent of a classical entablature, divided into architrave, frieze and cornice. It is probably related to a small group of triple fireplaces in France, the earliest installed in the great hall of the Palais de Justice in Poitiers, for Jean, duke of Berry, between 1384–6. The lintel of the Poitiers example can also be read as an entablature, raising the possibility that the Linlithgow fireplace formed part of James I's original scheme.[31] However, fireplaces with entablature-type remained popular in France well beyond the fifteenth century, so that the Lyon Chalmer fireplace could equally derive from Poitiers and still date from James IV's remodelling, without appearing old-fashioned. What distinguishes it from French examples are its sobriety and substitution of right angles for curves at the corners, which make it resemble more closely Italian fireplaces, such as those in the Salone del Trono in the ducal palace at Urbino, dating from the 1470s and attributed to Francesco di Giorgio. Even if the details of the Linlithgow fireplace are not as archaeologically correct as those at Urbino, they do stand comparison with the drawings in Francesco's *Saluzziano Codex* (c. 1480), where the details of the entablatures are more summary.[32]

All this begs the question of how could such influences have reached Scotland so early. The most obvious way would be the importation of Italian craftsmen, and there was an Italian mason in royal service in 1510–11. The works are unspecified, but, as the date coincides with the roofing of the Great Hall at Edinburgh Castle, it seems reasonable to link him with its unequivocally Italianate roof brackets.[33] Their style suggests familiarity with the works of Francesco di Giorgio or Filarete, known either from their buildings in Urbino or Milan or from copies of their treatises, and it is quite possible that James III and James IV had knowledge of one or both of them as we shall see below.

The presence of an Italian craftsman in the service of James IV is not so surprising given the Italophile nature of his own and his father's courts. James III wanted to visit Rome and appeared on 'the earliest Renaissance coin portrait outside Italy'.[34] However, a link more substantial than vague royal Italophilia is necessary to support the argument for a close connection between Linlithgow Palace and those buildings in Italy where we have identified parallels, and we have one in the person of Anselm Adornes, a Brugeois merchant of Genoese extraction.

James III befriended Adornes on his first visit to Scotland in 1468–9, and made him a knight and a member of his council. In 1470–1, Adornes journeyed to Jerusalem with his son, Jean, who wrote two accounts of the journey, an official version, the *Itinerarium*, which was dedicated to James III and presented to him by Anselm in 1471–2, and another, more personal in tone, written shortly before Jean's death in 1510.[35]

Jean and Anselm's outward and return journeys passed through Italy, where they visited most of the significant towns. The account shows a particular interest in fortifications, which sometimes spills over into civil and sacred architecture. Thus in Milan, the Castello Sforzesco is described, where Anselm met the duke and where Filarete's treatise was housed. He also saw Filarete's 'sumptuosissimum' Ospedale Maggiore. The Castello Visconteo in Pavia is described as 'a very beautiful and large castle, square with a great tower at each side and a park behind'. In Florence, the Palazzo Medici and the Palazzo Pazzi-Quaratesi are named, the former judged 'magnificent'. No details are given of what they saw in Rome, but during their first stay, Anselm had several private audiences with Paul II, while on their second visit they spent eighteen days, 'seeing daily the wonderful buildings and the ruins of the city'.[36]

Even though most of the details of Italy north of Rome were not in the version of the *Itinerarium* presented to James III, Anselm would have had ample opportunity to discuss the architectural wonders of Italy with the king, not just when he delivered the manuscript, but even more so after 1477, when he moved to Scotland and was made keeper of Linlithgow Palace.[37] No one was in a better position to effect its transformation *all'italiana* to something akin to both Filarete's designs and the Palazzo Venezia, then the most prestigious palace in Italy. While we can only conjecture that, given his evident interest in architecture, he may have seen the copy of Filarete's treatise in the Castello Sforzesco, we can be certain that he saw the Palazzo Venezia. Not only was it the largest construction project in Rome at the time, but it was also acting as a papal palace for Paul II.[38] Also explained are the reflections of the Castello Visconteo at Pavia in the form of Linlithgow, both square with towers at each corner and with parks behind, and of the portals of Florentine palaces in the windows of Linlithgow.

Even after Anselm's murder in 1483, seemingly because of resentment at his familiarity with James III, cultural contact between Italy and the Scottish court remained strong.[39] James IV spoke Italian, employed an Italian alchemist and musicians, and received gifts from three popes.[40] He also sent two of his sons, Alexander, archbishop of St Andrews, and Robert, earl of Moray, to study at Padua in 1507–8, where Erasmus became their tutor. In late 1508, Erasmus accompanied Alexander to Ferrara, Bologna and Florence en route to Siena, where the latter remained three months. Alexander rejoined Erasmus in Rome at Easter, 1509, and both then proceeded to Cumae, near Naples, before Alexander returned to Scotland.[41] Thus, just as Linlithgow was nearing completion, James IV could have learnt from his own son of the latest developments in Italian architecture.

It is now clear that, by 1513, Linlithgow was a highly eclectic work, incorporating features of planning and style from France, Flanders, and possibly, England, but, in both overall form and specific details, related most closely to comparable contemporary Italian signorial palaces. When one remembers that external details were freshly painted in strong colours and gilded in preparation for James V's marriage, and that the presently-exposed external rubble walls were almost certainly harled and possibly tinted, the palace must have made a spectacular show, and the reported words of Mary of Guise no longer seem hyperbolic.[42] That she was not alone in her admiration is suggested by striking similarities to Linlithgow in two of the most important Renaissance châteaux in France, namely Écouen and Ancy-le-Franc, two Danish royal castles, Kronborg and Frederiksborg, and two significant German *Schlösser*, Schloss Neuhaus and Aschaffenburg.

At Écouen, begun 1539, we find a symmetrical quadrangular plan, with four rectangular corner pavilions, for which there is no close French precedent.[43] Like Linlithgow, each of the pavilions has a spiral stair contained in a separate circular tower, although here they are sited in the angles between the projecting pavilions and the outer façades of the connecting south and north ranges rather than within the courtyard (Figure 1.5). This juxtaposition of spiral stairs in small round or square towers next to much larger rectangular pavilions has recently been recognised as an innovative compositional device, exploiting the differences in massing between the two elements.[44] The earliest French examples are the Château de Madrid and the Château Neuf at Fontainebleau, both dating from 1528, and Écouen is a prime specimen, but Linlithgow anticipates them by some twenty years. Another correspondence with Linlithgow found at Écouen is that its two entrances are guarded by small forestanding gates, for which again there is no obvious French precedent.

Sebastiano Serlio's château at Ancy-le-Franc, begun 1546 in a hybrid Franco–Italian idiom, also shares several features with Linlithgow.[45] Besides the correspondence of the quadrilateral plan with square towers, there are also spiral stairs at each corner of the court-yard, and two galleries facing each other across the courtyard, analogous to what is likely to have been the original arrangement at Linlithgow (Figure 1.6).[46] Thus, in several aspects, both Écouen and Ancy resemble Linlithgow more closely than possible French precedents. That their elevations are very different from the latter is not a problem, since it was accepted practice in the sixteenth century to borrow only the plan, as at Hardwick and Wollaton Halls, where the plans are adapted from Palladio, Serlio and Du Cerceau.[47]

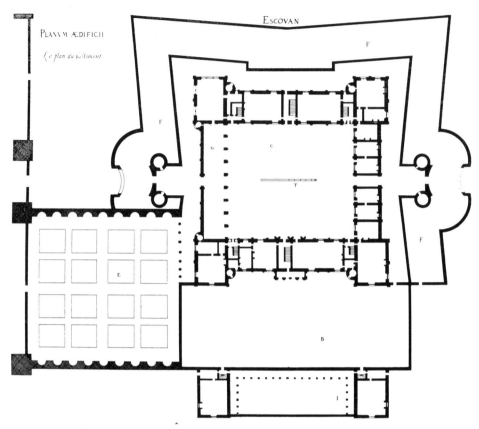

1.5 Château of Écouen, France, 1539 and later, plan. (Du Cerceau)

The builder of Écouen was Anne, duc de Montmorency, Constable of France, François I's great favourite, while the builder of Ancy was Antoine de Clermont-Tonnerre, brother-in-law to Diane de Poitiers, mistress of Henri II.[48] Thus, both were prominent at court, where also Serlio was resident from 1541, and would have been well-placed to learn of Linlithgow, since contact between the French and Scottish courts was strong in the first half of the sixteenth century, reaching a peak when James V came to France in 1536–7 to marry his first bride, Madeleine de Valois, daughter of François I, who died forty days after arriving in Scotland. Besides contact at the level of patrons, such as James himself, and courtiers such as Ronsard (who visited Linlithgow twice), there were also direct artistic contacts.[49] James took Moses Martin, a French mason already long in royal service in Scotland, to France with him to recruit compatriots to work in Scotland. The following year John Drummond, James' principal carpenter and artillery expert, spent several months in France. Letters also survive from the Duchess of Guise in 1539, advising her daughter, Mary, that she had engaged Nicholas Roy to come to Scotland with some companions.[50] Thus, there was considerable

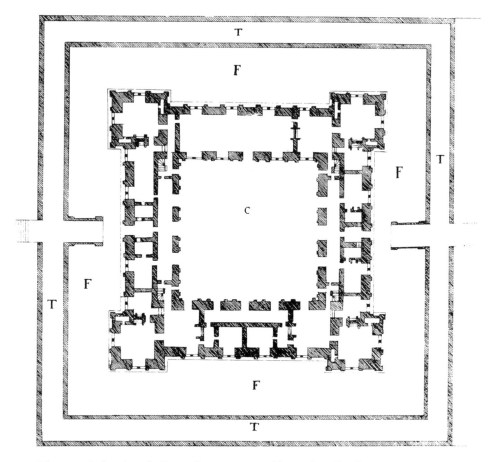

1.6 Sebastiano Serlio, Ancy-le-Franc, France, 1546 and later, plan. (Du Cerceau)

interchange between masons and craftsmen employed at the French and Scottish courts, just before Écouen and Ancy were begun. Clearly, the patrons and designers of Écouen and Ancy-le-France would have had little difficulty in gaining information on Linlithgow.

Another country where the influence of Linlithgow is evident is Denmark. Contacts between it and Scotland were strong throughout the fifteenth and sixteenth centuries, as demonstrated by the marriages of James III to Margaret of Denmark in 1469, and of James VI to Anne of Denmark in 1589.

In 1574, Anne's father, King Frederick II, began converting a medieval stronghold at Elsinore, known as the Krogen, into a palace, renamed Kronborg. This involved incorporating several separate buildings disposed around three sides of a quadrangle into continuous wings and building a new east wing to complete the enclosure of the courtyard by the late 1580s (Figure 1.7).[51] A fire in 1629, which caused extensive damage, makes it difficult to be sure of some details of Frederick's II scheme but, in overall conception, the palace bears a

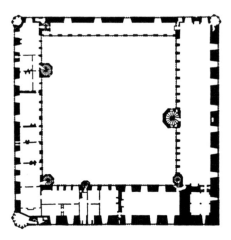

1.7 Kronborg, Elsinore, Denmark, 1574 and later, plan. (Arkitektens Verlag)

striking similarity to Linlithgow, and, again, it is difficult to find a closer precedent. All four corners have towers, turnpikes occupy two of the courtyard corners, and the façades were unusually faced with sandstone from Sweden rather than native Danish brick. The detailed treatment of the elevations look more to the Low Countries, reflecting the Flemish and Netherlandish origins of the principal named masons, but there is evidence of Scottish involvement.[52] Scots and their descendants were the most important group of foreigners resident in Elsinore in the late sixteenth century, and two of its members, the mayor, Frederick Lyall, and a town councillor, David Hansen, were in charge of the administration of the construction of Kronborg, which may have given them opportunity to influence the plan.[53]

Linlithgow's influence may also be detected at Christian IV's (brother-in-law to James VI) new country palace, Frederiksborg, built 1602–23.[54] Although it reverts to the typical Danish brick with stone dressings for its elevations, again in Flemish Renaissance style, so that the superficial similarity is not so obvious, the plan and overall form again resembles Linlithgow. It approximates to a square with three four-storey and one single-storey wings, closer in proportion and symmetry to Linlithgow than Kronborg. Another parallel with Linlithgow is the presence of a fountain, although here it stands in the forecourt to the palace.[55]

In this case, the influence of Linlithgow on Frederiksborg is probably indirect via Kronborg, but it is worth noting that James VI's master of works, William Schaw, accompanied the king to Denmark in 1589–90, and no doubt met his Danish counterparts, and that cultural relations between Scotland and Denmark were at their peak from then until 1603.[56]

The third area where Linlithgow may have exerted an influence is Germany, where several sixteenth- and early seventeenth-century *Schlösser* have quadrangular plans with turnpikes in the corner of the courtyards, two of which strongly recall Linlithgow. The first, begun in the 1520s, is Schloss Neuhaus (Figure 1.8), just north of Paderborn in Westphalia, built for

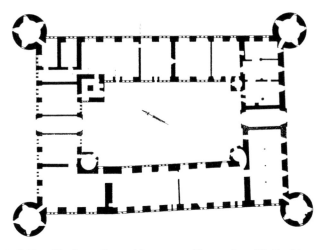

1.8 Jörg Unkair, Schloss Neuhaus, Detmold, 1520s and later, plan. (H. Kreft)

Erich of Brunswick-Grubenhagen, prince-bishop of Paderborn, by the mason, Jörg Unkair.[57] It is the earliest German *Schloss* to include Renaissance traits, such as paired rectangular windows, a feature common in Scotland, as in the great hall of Stirling Castle or the chapel at Falkland Palace. The plan is roughly rectangular with turnpikes to each corner of the three-storey courtyard. Two are hexagonal and identical, and two square of differing size, of which the larger probably dates from the 1590s. As originally built there were non-projecting square towers at the corners, but in the 1590s, circular pavilions were added at the angles, giving it now a very French appearance, and disguising the original similarity to Linlithgow.

The second example is the Schloss Johannisburg at Aschaffenburg, east of Mainz, 'the most considerable surviving secular work of the seventeenth century in Germany', built 1605–14, for Johann Schweickhardt von Kronberg, the archbishop-elector of Mainz, by the architect, Georg Ridinger.[58] The square courtyard is enclosed by four three-storey wings with identical turnpikes, square at ground level and polygonal above, with square towers projecting slightly at all four corners (Figure 1.9). The regularity of the design is only disturbed by the retained medieval keep on one side, but otherwise the resemblance of the plan to Linlithgow is strong, and closer than to other possible models, such as Ancy-le-Franc or the Danish palaces.

Scots were plentiful in Germany in the early sixteenth century, but there is no evidence to link them even tenuously with Neuhaus.[59] For the Johannisburg, however, we know for certain that its builder, Johannes Schweickhart, archbishop of Mainz 1604–26, had contact with Scots. Within his diocese lay St James, Erfurt, and within his metropolitan province, St James, Würzburg, two of the three Schottenklöster, monasteries originally founded by Irish monks, which passed into the control of a Scottish Benedictine congregation during the sixteenth century.[60] It is very likely that the abbot of Erfurt would have met the arch-

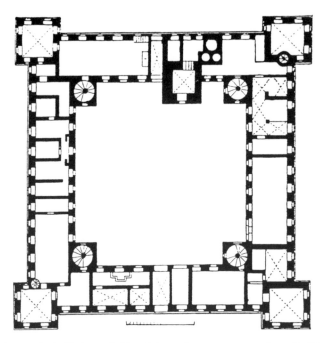

1.9 Georg Ridinger, Aschaffenburg, Schloss Johannisburg, 1605–14, plan. (R. Klapheck)

bishop, and official correspondence survives between the abbot of the third Schottenklöster, St James, Regensburg (the head of the congregation) and Johannes, while the Johannisburg was building.[61] Certainly, a predecessor of Johannes, Daniel Brendel von Homburg (archbishop, 1555–82) met Ninian Winzet, abbot of Regensburg (1577–92), who before the Scottish Reformation had been master of the grammar school and a chaplain of St Michael's, adjacent to the palace in Linlithgow.[62] Thus, yet again we have potential sources of information on Linlithgow in the circle of a patron at or shortly before a building with close parallels is erected.

To sum up, we have seen that Linlithgow Palace was transformed under James III and James IV into an Italianate palace, unparalleled in northern Europe for a generation. It thus became an object worthy of admiration for foreigners, with its plan imitated in France, Denmark and Germany. That these buildings were copying Linlithgow rather than examples of convergent evolution is suggested by the fact that in five out of six cases, Scots, some with personal knowledge of Linlithgow, moved in the circles of their builders, immediately before or during building. Such a scenario has profound implications for our understanding of Renaissance architecture in Scotland. Rather than dismissing it as a late development, derived via France, we can now see Scotland as precociously advanced and an exporter and interpreter of Italianate architectural ideas to other north Europeans.

Edinburgh College of Art

ACKNOWLEDGEMENTS

I am very pleased to acknowledge the assistance in various ways of the following: John Dunbar, John Macgregor, Charles McKean, Arnold Nesselrath, Geoffrey Stell, David Thomson and, above all, Miles Glendinning and Aonghus McKechnie, whose generosity in sharing information and insights has been unstinting.

NOTES

1. See Robert Lindsay of Pitscottie, *The Chronicles of Scotland*, ed. J. G. Dalyell, Edinburgh, 1814, p. 378: '... his grace [James V] cam to his awin pallace in Linlithgow, and remained ane day or twa, quhilk pallace the queine [Mary of Guise] highlie commendit, saying, shoe nevir sa a more princlie pallace'. Pitscottie (*c*.1532–*c*.1580) was writing in the later sixteenth century: see the standard edition, *The Historie and Cronicle of Scotland*, ed. A. J. G. Mackay, 3 vols, Edinburgh and London, 1899–1901, vol. 1, p. xxxiv–xli. Mary's remark is not found at the relevant place in this edition (ibid., p. 381), because Mackay relies on what he considers to be the oldest extant copy of Pitscottie's lost original (Mackay's Ms. A, Edinburgh University Library, Ms. La. III, p. 218), dating to the late sixteenth century (ibid., pp. lxii, lxxii–iii). However, this manuscript in places lacks material found in others, and the remark is found in most other versions, including the next oldest, dating from the early seventeenth century, Mackay's Ms. B, Edinburgh University Library, Ms. La. III 216, fol. 87v. (on Ms. B, see ibid., pp. lxxiv–v). For paraphrases, see, for example, Gordon Donaldson, *James V to James VII*, Edinburgh, 1965, pp. 57–8: '... at Linlithgow he [James V] raised a palace which Mary of Guise thought worthy of comparison with those of France'; and Rosalind K. Marshall, *Mary of Guise*, London, 1977, p. 64: 'It was, she declared, as fine as anywhere in France'.

2. Some of this argument is rehearsed in a wider context in Ian Campbell, 'A romanesque revival and the early Renaissance in Scotland *c*.1380–1513', *Journal of the Society of Architectural Historians*, 54: 3, forthcoming September 1995. For a conventional account, see Richard Fawcett, *Scottish Architecture from the Accession of the Stewarts to the Reformation 1371–1560* (Architectural History of Scotland, gen. eds Charles McKean and Deborah Howard), Edinburgh, 1994, pp. 320–30.

3. Ibid., pp. 101–2; Michael Brown, *James I*, Edinburgh, 1994, pp. 114–15; Denys Pringle, *Linlithgow Palace: a Historical Guide to the Royal Palace and Peel*, Edinburgh, 1989, pp. 6–7; and Royal Commission on Ancient and Historical Monuments of Scotland (RCAHMS), *Tenth Report with Inventory of Monuments and Constructions in the Counties of Midlothian and West Lothian*, Edinburgh, 1929, p. 220. For the first use of the term 'palace' for Linlithgow, see *The Exchequer Rolls of Scotland*, ed. John Stuart et al., 23 vols, Edinburgh, 1878–1908, vol. 4, p. 513.

4. Fawcett, *Scottish Architecture*, p. 304; Pringle, *Linlithgow Palace*, p. 9; and RCAHMS, *West Lothian*, fig. 275. The lack of surviving records from the last

years of James III's reign makes it difficult to know for certain what was happening at Linlithgow, but the fact that we do have records of building works there from the very first year of James IV's reign strongly suggests that a campaign was already under way rather than that he initiated them immediately on accession: see Pringle, *Linlithgow Palace*, p. 10. Christopher Wilson, 'Linlithgow Palace', in Colin McWilliam, *Lothian (except Edinburgh)* (Buildings of Scotland), Harmondsworth, 1978, finds the accounts too patchy and confusing and relies on stylistic and archaeological evidence for his datings (see p. 293).

5. Fawcett, *Scottish Architecture*, pp. 304–10; Pringle, *Linlithgow Palace*, p. 11; and RCAHMS, *West Lothian*, pp. 223–4.

6. Fawcett, *Scottish Architecture*, pp. 325–7; Pringle, *Linlithgow Palace*, pp. 14–15; Charles McKean, 'Finnart's Platt', *Architectural Heritage*, 1991, vol. 2, pp. 3–17 (pp. 8–9); RCAHMS, *West Lothian*, p. 225; and Henry M. Paton (ed.) *Accounts of the Masters of Works for Building and Repairing Royal Palaces and Castles: Volume 1 1529–1615*, Edinburgh, 1957, pp. 115–31.

7. Pringle, *Linlithgow Palace*, pp. 19–22.

8. RCAHMS, *West Lothian*, p. 221, notes that with James IV's works 'the palace became a symmetrical study both in plan and elevation – an unusually early application in Scotland of symmetrical composition'.

9. Fawcett, *Scottish Architecture*, p. 306, suggests that the original purpose of the Bulwark was to buttress the north-east corner of the palace, which perhaps was already showing signs of the instability, which led to the collapse of the north quarter in 1607. This would certainly explain its eccentric siting, which seems inconsistent with the rest of James IV's works. There is no physical evidence that it ever stretched across the entire façade, even if that may have been intended.

10. Ibid., p. 301; and Wilson, 'Linlithgow Palace', pp. 291–2.

11. Brown, *James I*, p. 40.

12. John G. Dunbar, 'French influence in Scottish architecture during the sixteenth century', *Scottish Records Association Conference Paper*, vol. 12 (September, 1989), pp. 3–8 (p. 3); and Wilson, 'Linlithgow Palace', p. 294. Wilson refers to the similarity in treatment of the east gateway of Linlithgow to La Ferté-Milon. Fawcett, however (*Scottish Architecture*, p. 308), suggests that the gateway was remodelled by James IV and relates it to Louis XII's gate at Blois. While the flanking tabernacles do seem to be later additions, the parallel with Blois seems less convincing than the similarities to La Ferté-Milon.

13. Jean Mesqui and Claude Ribéra-Pervillé, 'Les châteaux de Louis d'Orléans et leurs architectes 1391–1407', *Bulletin Monumental*, vol. 138, 1980, pp. 293–345. On Charles of Orleans etc., see Brown, *James I*, pp. 21–4.

14. Fawcett, *Scottish Architecture*, p. 30.

15. See Pringle, *Linlithgow Palace*, p. 11. The tracery of the ground-storey windows differs from those of the upper floors, which have the distinctive Scottish rounded arches with inset cusps (see Campbell, 'Romanesque

revival'). The ground-floor tracery is similar to a window at the west end of the north aisle of the nave of Dunkeld Cathedral, which dates from Brown's episcopate (1484–1515), and to the windows of the chapel of St Leonard's College, St Andrews, which probably date from *c.*1512, when the college was founded by Alexander Stewart, James IV's son: see McGibbon, *Ecclesiastical Architecture*, vol. 3, pp. 43 and 448; and Gifford, *Fife*, pp. 386–7.

16. A fragment of the original north quarter is exposed close to the turnpike in the north-east corner of the courtyard. Its elaborate mouldings, running vertically, are clearly the jamb of an aperture and closely resemble those of the courtyard entrance to the Lyon Chalmer, and therefore probably date from James IV's remodelling. It is difficult to imagine that the jamb formed part of a significant entrance to the upper floors, given its siting so close to another stair, and one therefore wonders if the aperture formed part of an open arcade on the side of the courtyard most exposed to the sun. On the Falkland gallery, see Stuart et al. *Exchequer Rolls*, vol. 7, p. 106, 'Expense ejusdem ... per ... clausura duarum camerarum in le galry ...'. The use of French suggests a French origin for the gallery. The earliest example discussed in Jean Guillaume's, 'Le Galerie dans le château Français: place et fonction', *Revue de l'Art*, 1993, pp. 32–42, is Le Plessis-Bourré which is later than Falkland. However, Pierre-Marie Auzas, in 'Le Château du Plessis-Bourré', *Congrès Archéologique*, 1964, pp. 252–63, suggests as a precedent for its gallery, that built at Blois, 1443–57 by Charles d'Orléans (ibid., p. 256). Nevertheless, Philip the Good's palaces in Bruges and Ghent featured galleries: see Simon Thurley, *The Royal Palaces of Tudor England: Architecture and Court Life 1460–1547*, New Haven and London, 1993, pp. 14–15. Both the Flemish and the Blois examples probably derived from Charles V's Hôtel Saint-Pol in Paris. On other Scottish galleries, see John G. Dunbar, 'Some aspects of the planning of Scottish royal palaces in the sixteenth century', *Architectural History*, vol. 27, 1984, pp. 15–24.

17. Fawcett, *Scottish Architecture*, p. 305; David Lindsay, *The Testament and Complaynt of the Papyngo*, vol. 11, pp. 638–9: 'Adew Lythquo, quhose palyce of pleasaunce / Mycht be one patrone in Portingall or France'; Douglas Hamer (ed.) *The Works of Sir David Lindsay of the Mount 1490–1555*, 4 vols (Scottish Text Society), Edinburgh and London, 1931–4, vol. 1, p. 75. The reference to Portugal is intriguing, as a Portuguese 'wright' was working at Linlithgow around 1507: see *Treasurer's Accounts*, vol. 4, p. 185. However, Lindsay's first known visit abroad is to Flanders in 1531, so that he is probably not writing from personal knowledge: see Carol Edington, *Sir David Lindsay of the Mount: Political and Religious Culture in Renaissance Scotland* (unpub. thesis, University of St Andrews, 1991), p. 58.

18. James S. Richardson and James Beveridge, *Linlithgow Palace, Lothian*, Edinburgh, 1948, p. 22.

19. On the Louvre, see Mary Whiteley, 'Le Louvre de Charles V: dispositions et fonctions d'une résidence royale', *Revue de l'Art*, vol. 97, 1992, pp. 60–71. For Plessis-Bourré, Wolfram Prinz and Ronald G. Kecks, *Das französische Schloß*

der Renaissance: Form und Bedeutung der Architektur, ihre geschichtlichen und gesellschaftlichen Grundlagen, Berlin, 1985, pp. 46–8; and André Mussat, 'Tradition militaire et plaisance dans la seconde moitié du xve siècle', in Le Château en France, ed. Jean Babelon, 2nd edn., Paris, 1988, pp. 121–32. Nothing in France compares with Linlithgow in regularity of plan before Verger (still with round towers), which dates from the end of the fifteenth century, by which time Linlithgow's overall form was determined: see Jean Pierre Babelon, Châteaux de France au Siècle de la Renaissance, Paris, 1989, pp. 37–8. On the turnpikes, compare that in the Cour d'Honneur at Tarascon in Provence, built around 1430: see Sylvia Pressouyre, 'Le Château de Tarascon', Congrès Archéologique, 1963, pp. 221–43 (p. 238).

20. See John White, Art and Architecture in Italy: 1250–1400, Harmondsworth, 1966, pp. 330–5.

21. On the 'palacium ad modum castri', see Antonio Nicoli, 'Il lungo autunno dei castelli estensi', in Rocche fortilizi castelli in Emilia Romagna Marche, ed. Giuseppe Adani, Cinisello Balsano, 1988, pp. 51–64 (p. 58). On the comparable use of features from military architecture in domestic architecture in England and France, see Charles Coulson, 'Structural symbolism in medieval castle architecture', Journal of the British Archaeological Association, vol. 132, 1979, pp. 73–90; 'Hierarchism in conventual crenellation', Medieval Archaeology, vol. 26, 1982, pp. 69–100; etc.

22. Antonio Filarete, Trattato d'architettura, 2 vols, ed. A. M. Finoli and L. Grassi, Milan, 1972, vol. 1, pp. 99–101, 114–15 and 146–8. Linlithgow appears to have had a small tower over the main entrance, like Filarete's ducal palace: see Campbell, 'Romanesque revival'.

23. See principally, Christoph L. Frommel, 'Francesco del Borgo, Architekt Pius'II. und Pauls II. 2: Palazzo Venezia, Palazzetto Venezia und S. Marco', Römisches Jahrbuch für Kunstgeschichte, vol. 21, 1984, pp. 71–164; also useful are Maria Letizia Casanova Uccella, Palazzo Venezia: Paolo II e le Fabbriche di San Marco, Rome, 1980, and Torgil Magnuson, Studies in Roman Quattrocento Architecture, Stockholm, 1958, pp. 245–96.

24. Frommel, 'Palazzo Venezia', pp. 126–7: '... questo superbissimo pallazo pontificale excedente de fabrica, de sito, de magnificentia molti e molti altri pallazi regali ...'. For the east façade, see ibid., pp. 138–9; on the parapet and tower, see ibid., p. 97.

25. The use of small round towers is found in James IV's works at the Stirling Forework, the Linlithgow Bulwark and for the gatehouses of Holyrood and Falkland palaces, but none is as large as contemporary French pavilions. The first realisation of the full quadrangular plan with circular corner pavilions in Scotland appears to be the temporary palace built by the Earl of Atholl in 1531 to receive James V. See McKean, 'Finnart's Platt', p. 8, but it seems to have been partly anticipated by the quadrangle of King's College, Aberdeen, largely complete by 1514, which had projecting circular towers to two of its corners: see Macfarlane, William Elphinstone and the Kingdom of Scotland 1431–1514, Aberdeen, 1985, p. 337, and the illustration in A Tribute Offered by the University

of Aberdeen to the Memory of William Kelly, LL.D., A.R.S.A., ed. William D.
Simpson, *Aberdeen University Studies*, no. 125, Aberdeen, 1949, fig. 31.

26. *Treasurer's Accounts*, vol. 4, p. 280.

27. Wilson, 'Linlithgow Palace', p. 297. RCAHMS (*West Lothian*, p. 230)
supports the 1530s dating, quoting *Masters of Works*, February 1534, vol. 1,
p. 128: 'Item to Thomas Peblis for the glasining of the fyve windois of the west
syd of the Lyon chalmer ...'. McKean too believes the Lyon Chalmer was
extensively refitted in the 1530s ('Finnart's Platt', pp. 8–9). Leaving aside the
fact that there are six windows on each side of the hall, it is clear from the
context of the rest of the accounts that the work is in connection with the
installation of painted glass in the hall windows and in the chapel, and that the
work is less extensive than that in 1511–12 (referred to in the previous note).
Over each of the hall windows are triangular marks, resembling the ghosts of
pediments, perhaps executed in timber. These marks deserve further
investigation.

28. RCAHMS, *West Lothian*, p. 225, and Pringle, *Linlithgow Palace*, p. 11. There
is a payment for battlements on the west range in 1504 in the *Treasurers'
Accounts*, vol. 2, p. 440. Wilson, 'Linlithgow Palace', pp. 300–1, argues that
the Roman style of the lettering of the royal cipher indicates a date in the
1530s. However, an identical cipher appears on a floor tile from Linlithgow,
accepted as dating from James IV's reign, and, conclusively, on the altar frontal
on an illuminated page of James IV's book of hours, now in Vienna. See James
S. Richardson, 'A thirteenth-century tile kiln at North Berwick, East Lothian
and Scottish mediaeval ornamental floor tiles', *Proceedings of the Society of
Antiquaries of Scotland* 1928–9, vol. 63, pp. 281–310, esp. pp. 308–9; and
Leslie Macfarlane, 'The Book of Hours of James IV and Margaret Tudor', *Innes
Review* 1960, vol. 11, pp. 3–21, esp. p. 13.

29. See Campbell 'Romanesque revival'.

30. See Babelon (ed.), *Châteaux*, pp. 110–18; and Marc-Hamilton Smith,
'François Ier, l'Italie et le Château de Blois', *Bulletin Monumental*, 1989, vol.
147, pp. 307–23. John Dunbar has remarked on similarities between the
François Ier wing and the east quarter of Falkland Palace in 'Some French
parallels', pp. 7–8; and in a personal communication (dated 2 February 1994)
notes that the oriels, which are such prominent and unusual features of the
Blois façade, are paralleled by two in a similar position on the north façade of
Linlithgow, which are part of James IV's works of *c.*1505, and hence anticipate
those at Blois by at least a decade.

31. L. Labande-Mailfert, 'Le Palais de Justice de Poitiers', *Congrès
Archéologique*, 1951, pp. 27–43 (p. 41); Philippe Chapu, 'Le décor intérieur du
château au Moyen Age', in Babelon (ed.), *Le Château*, pp. 168–78 (p. 171);
and Joan Evans, *Art in Mediaeval France 987–1498*, London, 1948, pp. 164–5.

32. Chapu, 'Le décor', p. 171; Pasquale Rotondi, *Il palazzo ducale di Urbino*,
2 vols, Urbino, 1950–1, vol. 1, p. 453, n. 195; Francesco di Giorgio Martini,
Trattati, 2 vols, ed. C. Maltese and L. Maltese Grassi, Milan, 1967, vol. 1, pl.
41. The Linlithgow lintel is certainly closer to a classical entablature than

Filarete's drawings of fireplaces: see Filarete, *Trattati*, vol. 2, pl. 44. The Poitiers fireplace may be taken as evidence of the first French Renaissance centred on the courts of Charles V and his sons, including Jean de Berry: see Louis Courajod, *Les Origines de la Renaissance en France au xive et xve siècles*, Paris, 1888, *passim*; and Arthur Tilley, *The Dawn of the French Renaissance*, Cambridge, 1918, pp. 56–8. The fireplace in James IV's private closet also has a cornice which appears classical.

33. See Dunbar, 'French influence', p. 4, and *Treasurers' Accounts*, vol. 4, p. 271, where he is named 'Cressent': there is another payment in 1512 to 'the Italian mason' (ibid., p. 43). A family of masons in royal service from the 1460s to the 1530s bore the non-native surname 'Merlioun', provoking speculation that they were French in origin. However, the name is not obviously French, and one is tempted to suggest that Merlioun sounds rather like 'Marliano', a name common in Lombardy: see Gifford, *Fife*, pp. 213 and 295; Dunbar, 'French influence', p. 4; RCAHMS, *Stirlingshire*, vol. 1, p. 183.

34. See Norman Macdougall, *James III: A Political Study*, Edinburgh, 1982, pp. 114–15; and Ian Halley Stewart, *The Scottish Coinage*, London, 1955, p. 67.

35. See Alan Macquarrie, 'Anselm Adornes of Bruges: traveller in the east and friend of James III', *Innes Review*, vol. 33, 1982, pp. 15–22; and Macquarrie, *Scotland and the Crusades*, pp. 97–100. The account of his travels is published as the *Itinéraire d'Anselme Adorno en Terre Sainte (1470–1471)*, ed. and tr. Jacques Heers and Georgette de Groer (Sources d'histoire médiévale publiées par l'Institut de Recherche et d'Histoire des Textes), Paris, 1978. James III's copy is lost and the only original manuscript surviving is in Lille (ibid., pp. 19–20): the more personal version is known only through an abridgement transcribed by Edmond de la Coste: *Anselme Adorno, sire de Corthuy, pèlerin de Terre Sainte*, Brussels, 1855. Divergences from the Lille manuscript are reprinted in the *Itinéraire*.

36. For Milan, see ibid., pp. 434–8; for Pavia, see ibid., p. 442: 'castrum pulcerrimum, quadrum et magnum, in quolibet latere habens magnam turrim. Potest quidem castrum illud eques armatus lancea erecta usque ad altum ascendere. Retro castrum est parcus, sive lucus in circuitu miliaria … viginti quod circum muratum est'; for Florence, and for Rome, ibid., pp. 41 and 480: '[Roman] ubi persansimus bene per 18 dies, videntes dietim miranda edificia et ruinas urbis que vere demiranda sunt'.

37. Macquarrie, 'Anselm Adornes', p. 20. The reason given for not going into detail about Rome north of Italy is that James knew enough of these places because his subjects were so frequent visitors there: *Itinéraire*, p. 38.

38. Ibid., p. 41: on Palazzo Venezia as a papal palace, see Magnuson, *Roman Quattrocento Architecture*, p. 262.

39. Macquarrie, 'Anselm Adornes', pp. 20–1.

40. Macdougall, *James IV*, is the standard work. See also Ronald Nicholson, *Scotland: The Later Middle Ages*, Edinburgh, 1989, pp. 576–606; and Michael Lynch, *Scotland: A New History*, London, 1992, pp. 158–62. On the papal gifts, see Charles J. Burnett and Christopher J. Tabraham, *The Honours of Scotland:*

The Story of the Scottish Crown Jewels, Edinburgh, 1993, pp. 17–18; and Charles Burns, 'The Golden Rose and the blessed sword', *Innes Review*, vol. 20, 1969, pp. 150–94.

41. John Herkless and Robert K. Hannay, *The Archbishops of St Andrews*, 5 vols, Edinburgh, 1907–15, vol. 1, pp. 231–49; and Augustin Reynaudet, *Erasme et l'Italie*, Geneva, 1954, pp. 87–90. During his time in Padua, a now lost copy of Francesco di Giorgio's first treatise was being executed, and while in Siena, he had the opportunity to visit the nearby abbey of Monte Oliveto Maggiore, still then the home of Francesco di Giorgio's Ashburnham and Saluzziano codices: see Gustina Scaglia, *Francesco di Giorgio: Checklist and History of Manuscripts and Drawings*, New York and London, 1992, pp. 25, 31 and 185, no. 76.

42. For painting and gilding, see *Masters of Works*, vol. 1, p. 128. For harling in general, see Charles McKean, 'The Scottishness of Scottish architecture', in *Scotland: A Concise Cultural History*, ed. Paul H. Scott, Edinburgh, 1993, pp. 228–52 (p. 237). The gilded finials of Holyrood and pediments of James VI's palace at Edinburgh Castle give us a hint of what was intended, but when one reads that the ironwork of windows at Linlithgow was painted vermilion, one begins to realise that the original effect must have been stunning. Gavin Douglas' allegorical poem, 'The palice of Honour' (c.1501), dedicated to James IV, describes a castellated palace, magnificently ornamented with gilded towers, turnpikes, bejewelled mouldings etc., which he probably based on Linlithgow, as the largest Scottish royal palace: see 'The palice of Honour', 11. 1429–46, in *The Shorter Poems of Gavin Douglas*, ed. Priscilla J. Bawcutt (Scottish Text Society), Edinburgh and London, 1967, p. 92.

43. See Babelon, *Châteaux*, pp. 329–38.

44. See Jean Guillaume, 'L'Escalier dans l'architecture française de la première moitié du XVIème siècle', in *L'Escalier dans l'Architecture de la Renaissance: Actes du Colloque Tenus a Tours du 22 au 26 mai 1979*, Paris, 1985, pp. 27–45 (pp. 36–7).

45. See Babelon, *Châteaux*, pp. 384–93; and Sabine Kühbacher, 'Il problema di Ancy-le-Franc', in *Sebastiano Serlio* (Sesto seminario internazionale di storia dell'architettura: Vicenza 31 agosto – 4 settembre 1987), ed. Christof Thoenes, Milan, 1989, pp. 79–91.

46. It is true that the stairs are not expressed externally, but Guillaume drew attention to drawings, which he believed to be a project for Ancy, which do show the stairs projecting in towers into the corners of the courtyard and above the wall head of the main ranges. See Jean Guillaume, 'Serlio est-il l'architecte d'Ancy-le-Franc?: À propos d'un dessin inédit de la Bibliothèque Nationale', *Revue de l'Art*, vol. 5, 1969, pp. 9–18 (p. 15). It is now realised that the drawings are after Project XXVI of Du Cerçeau, which David Thomson has described as a 'pastiche' Ancy: Jacques Androuet du Cerçeau, *Les Plus Excellents Bastiments de France*, ed. David Thomson, Paris, 1988, pp. 140–3. Ancy is not the only case where Serlio appears to have been anticipated by Scottish buildings: a woodcut in Serlio's *Third Book* (1537) is very similar to the gateway of James IV's Forework at Stirling Castle: see Campbell, 'Romanesque revival'.

47. John Summerson, *Architecture in Britain 1530–1830*, Harmondsworth, 1970, pp. 68 and 71; and David Thomson, 'France's earliest illustrated printed architectural pattern book: Designs for living "à la française" of the 1540s', in *Architecture et Vie Sociale: L'Organisation Intérieure des Grandes Demeures à la Fin du Moyen Age et à la Renaissance: Actes du Colloque Tenu à Tours du 6 au 10 Juin 1988*, Paris, 1994, pp. 221–33 (p. 225).

48. Babelon, *Châteaux*, pp. 332 and 384.

49. On Ronsard in Scotland, see Michel Simonin, *Pierre de Ronsard*, Mesnil-sur-l'Estrée, 1990, 64–77.

50. On Martin and French masons brought over by James V, see John G. Dunbar, 'French influence in Scottish Architecture', pp. 4–5; and *Masters of Works*, pp. xxxiii–iv. On Drummond, see *Masters of Works*, p. xxxvi.

51. Jorgen Sestoft and Jorgen Hegner Christiansen, *Guide to Danish Architecture I: 1000–1960*, Copenhagen, 1991, pp. 78–9; and Joakim Skovgaard, *A King's Architecture: Christian IV and his Buildings*, London, 1973, pp. 17–20.

52. Skovgaard, *King's Architecture*, pp. 17–18.

53. Thomas Riis, *Should Auld Acquaintance Be Forgot ...: Scottish–Danish Relations c. 1450–1707*, 2 vols, Odense, 1988, vol. 1, pp. 171–2; vol. 2, pp. 216 and 231.

54. Sestoft, *Danish Architecture*, p. 81; and Skovgaard, *King's Architecture*, pp. 45–58.

55. Kronborg originally had a fountain in its courtyard, but it was removed during the Swedish occupation of 1658–60: André Leth, *Kronborg: The Castle and the Royal Apartments*, s.l., 1978, p. 6.7.

56. Riis, *Auld Acquaintance*, vol. 1, pp. 121–30; vol. 2, p. 73.

57. Henry-Russell Hitchcock, *German Renaissance Architecture*, Princeton, 1981, pp. 49–52.

58. Ibid., pp. 285–7; see also Friedrich Mulke, 'Les Escaliers allemands de la fin du Moyen Age et de la Renaissance', in *L'Escalier*, pp. 189–206 (p. 191).

59. Theodor A. Fischer, *The Scots in Germany: Being a Contribution towards the History of the Scot Abroad*, Edinburgh, 1902.

60. Mark Dilworth, *The Scots in Franconia*, Edinburgh and London, 1974, pp. 18–39.

61. Ibid., pp. 46–7.

62. Ibid., pp. 23–31.

JOHN G. HARRISON

The Toun's New House: An Early Georgian Development in Stirling

In 1719 Stirling town council undertook to develop the site of the ruinous Garden's Old Lodging, near the Mercat Cross. The Toun's New House had four shops on the ground floor; the upper floors were rented for commercial and residential use. It was a prestige project, to an initial design apparently by Scotland's leading architects. Council decisions, building accounts and an inventory of fixtures provide unusual detail about construction, use and decoration. In 1924 the property was surveyed by the Office of Works with a view to modernisation and preservation but the scheme was rejected and the property demolished.

LIKE OTHER TOWN COUNCILS, Stirling owned and periodically repaired or rebuilt a variety of buildings, including the Manse, Hangman's House, Grammar School, Corn Exchange, Tolbooth and mills. At various times between 1660 and 1705 other Stirling institutions (Spittal's Hospital, the Fleshers, the Weavers) invested funds in existing houses whilst the Incorporated Trades bought Lawrie's Turnpike in 1712, combining a meeting hall and housing for rent. There is some evidence of other contemporary Scots urban institutions investing in property as a source of income about this time but the Toun's New House was unusual if not unique as an early example of building municipal housing for rent. The council refused to grant the site of the derelict Garden's Old Lodging to the merchant guildry for development and undertook the work itself.[1]

It was a controversial scheme, pursued with a near reckless disregard for expense. The total costs exceeded £15,000 (Scots), of which £8,537 was borrowed in 1718–19 at 4.5 per cent interest; the rent paid on the finished building came to a mere £426 per annum or less than a 3 per cent return on capital, even if the considerable costs of maintenance are ignored. Sale of the property in 1741 raised only £7,260. All major votes concerning the development were contested and one was reversed. Probably the whole lavish scheme was the idea of a small group or even of an enthusiastic individual, able to manipulate a normally parsimonious council.[2]

Contemporary Stirling councils certainly encouraged fashionable developments, of which the Tolbooth (1703–5), designed by Sir William Bruce, was the most notable. In 1718 the council granted the Weavers a cash subsidy to insert sash windows in their house 'for the decorment of the ... public street', in 1724 they waived debts owed by Clerk Don on account of 'the great decorment' made by his 'spacious lodging' and in 1732 'considering how much the foir street is decorated' by a new house, they gave two guineas (Sterling) to the master mason.[3]

The council's first interest is recorded on 8 November 1718 and the following February it was decided to commission architectural drawings from 'Mr McGill, architek'; however the accounts show final payment for plans to have been to 'Mr Smith'. James Smith and Alexander McGill were the foremost architects in Scotland at this time. They worked on a number of projects together in the early eighteenth century, although their partnership came to an end around 1719.

McGill had designed a new layout for the Stirling courtroom in 1709 and in 1726 he was to advise the council on deepening the fords on the Forth. Smith must have known the town well and both he and McGill were honorary merchant-guildbrethren of Stirling. Smith is assumed to have designed Smith's Land or Close in Edinburgh but otherwise neither man is credited with tenement blocks.

The plans, which cost £76 16s. (Scots) do not survive. There is no evidence that either man visited the site and detailed day-to-day supervision was by the Burgh Treasurer whilst the council continued to vote on details of construction and decoration as building proceeded. A proposal on 29 August 1719 that 'ane tympan should be built on the fore front of the towns house … for the greater decorment thereof' was carried, if only 'by plurality of voices'; but on 10 September, finding that 'the same would prejudge the roof' the council ordered the roof 'to be put on in a plain way without flankers which the tympan would occasion.' This and other resolutions suggest that there could have been considerable deviation from the original plans.

In May 1719, before the draft plans were agreed, discussions were held with Forrester of Logie, joint owner of the eastern gable, who was allowed to put in new windows, in compensation for his inevitable loss of rent during the work. There is no evidence of a written contract for the work and approval on 12 September 1719 of the expenditure of £38 10s. for ale in Mrs Burgess's house at a meeting with the 'measons, borrowmen and officers about the new house' implies that discussions and verbal agreement were deemed sufficient. A final decision to go ahead was made in July 1719 and by March 1720 the main building was so nearly complete that the windows had been glazed.

Leases were granted to the upper two floors and the attics from 15 May 1720. Communal midden steadings and coal houses were included in the original scheme but, in December 1720, it was decided to add a stable, brewhouse, ale and wine cellars, all to be let to the tenant of the still-vacant first floor which was let the next week to George Henderson, a sequence of events implying that the additions were built to secure Henderson's anticipated entry.

On the ground floor were the central entry and four shops each with fore and back rooms; the four tenants of the upper floors each rented a shop. A central close led to a stair to the rear. The first floor probably had eight to ten apartments. The second and third floors were each divided between two tenants, who probably occupied four rooms and a kitchen each, with shared use of the garret floor. This was probably a typical arrangement for early eighteenth-century Stirling, where ground floors were often used as 'cellars', for storage, as brewhouses, stables etc. (Figures 2.1–2.3).

However, differing from most recorded seventeenth-century Stirling tenements, the architects and masons were sufficiently confident to abandon traditional barrel vaulting of the ground floors. And though the staircase was built outside the walls of the main building, the traditional spiral turnpike was abandoned in favour of a platt and scale stair.

The shops and all the residential apartments and stairs (but not the garrets) were lathed and plastered, including plaster ceilings with wooden cornices in the residential rooms. A payment for 'whitening the Town's New House' in 1721 could refer to external work but more likely to room painting. All shops and rooms were fitted with iron fire grates (known as chimneys); 'kitchen chimneys', specially adapted for cooking, in each kitchen and 'chamber chimneys' in other rooms.[4] Each kitchen had a box bed. The shops had floors of 'pavement' whilst upper floors were of nailed boards. The front windows were glazed with crown glass and the rear ones with 'common glass' and some (perhaps only the front) were sash windows for which lead 'paces' [paises are weights], pulleys and tows were provided.

The plastering of ceilings and walls was a particular mark of comfort and modernity and one requiring specific authorisation from the council. These were features still being put into prestigious older Stirling properties such as the Manse and the Friers' [sic] House, as they were modernised, bringing new standards of privacy and insulation. Sash windows were a similar prestigious innovation, reducing draughts and enhancing appearance.[5] The insertion of sash windows into the Weavers' House has already been mentioned; a payment of £1 8s. to William Smith for 'a pace to the Council House Windows' in 1720–1 implies that sashes may have been fitted there either as part of Bruce's 1703–5 work or as part of McGill's 1709 re-design. The front (south-facing) rooms of the New House with their numerous, large windows and plastered ceilings must have been enviably bright, cheerful and warm.

The rents charged and the social profile of the tenants confirms the prestigious nature of the project. George Henderson paid £162 (Scots) per year at a time when Stirling houses could still be rented for well under £10. Within a short time of his entering, the council began to hold many of their official functions in his house and Fleming asserts that the premises were a hotel. Each of the other tenants paid a substantial £66 per annum. One tenant was a merchant and dyster, one a general merchant, whilst John Hyndshaw was a stationer and bookbinder as well as a merchant guild member. Andrew Millar's occupation is unclear. Prior to new leases being granted in 1731, offerers had to promise not to carry out 'any noisome work within or without the doors'; again, all the tenants, including Henderson who renewed his lease, were of high status.[6]

As with other urban developments, the stones of the previous building were re-used, as far as possible. Part of the balance was made up of thirteen boat-loads of dressed freestone

2.1 James Smith and Alexander McGill, 'The Toun's New House', Broad Street, Stirling, 1719, main elevation. (Dryesdale's *Auld Stirling Biggins*)

2.2 An unusual rear view of the building, showing some of the office houses. (Dryesdale's *Auld Stirling Biggins*)

from Longannet. The Old Statistical Account for Tulliallan says the Longannet quarry was 'in great reputation, time immemorial' and stone was shipped to Edinburgh and even, perhaps, to Amsterdam. Its use in this project is another indicator of prestige; transport added £429 to the £489 cost of quarrying and dressing. Undressed stone from the Black Craig (unlocated) cost a further £171 including transport. Adam Jack's charge of £1,214 for skailzie [mud-stone slates] for roofing includes his labour costs. Sand, brought from the sandpits just south of the town, cost £144. Lime cost £733, implying a purchase of over 100 chalders; such large quantities were usually 'boat lime' brought up river from Kinghorn, Limekilns or elsewhere on the northern shores of the Forth.[7]

Timber (including wainscot, 'tries' and deals) cost £4,409; most of it supplied by John and James Watson, long established as timber merchants in the town. The rest (some second hand) came from a variety of suppliers in Stirling and Alloa. Metal items cost £1,185, of which nails account for £413 whilst Colin McLourie, smith, charged £634 for a mixture of work tools, nails, locks, keys and chimneys (firegrates). The balance of the costs for metal goods went on such items as window bars (set in lead), a lead 'spout' and other minor items. All these items were of local manufacture, even the lead weights for the sash windows were

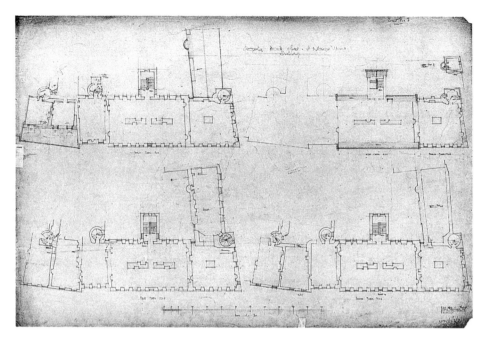

2.3 Plan of the building, 1924. (Crown copyright)

specially cast by a coppersmith. The other important manufactured item was glazing which cost £462 including labour costs. There were tiny costs for items such as glue, twine, rope etc.

Wages for 'on site' work totalled £5,128. The principal mason was Alexander Dollar, who was paid approximately £2,520 for his work on the main house. Two principal wrights were employed, John Gillespie and his workmen being paid £1,149 and John Christie and his men £386. All the principals were burgesses and regularly employed on council work around this period.

John Berrihill and James Harper, paid some £327 for plastering, deserve particular note. Francis Dyer is the only resident painter recorded in seventeenth-century Stirling and he was returned as 'poor' in the 1691 Hearth Tax. In 1700 John Berrihill 'painter from Alloa' was admitted as a burgess 'gratis', a common procedure to encourage men with particular skills to settle. By 1707 Berrihill was engaged in a furious argument with his apprentice, John Matheson, who a few years later was regularly working for the council. By 1720 there were at least 4 painter-plasterers working in Stirling, serving what was obviously a greatly expanded market for decorative skills.

Clearing up, barrowmen and other ancillary costs came to £745. Other minor costs brought the total expended on the main building to £15,416 (Scots).

All the new stone for the ancillary buildings came from the 'Black Craig' where it cost only £43, though transport cost £210; obviously, residual stone from the main building may also have been used. A massive 19,000 skailzie cost £456; they probably came from Knock-hill, Bridge of Allan. The lesser quantity of lime needed for this work came from the middle Bannock Burn area (North Third and Caldhame) and cost £115; sand cost £68. Purchase of 600 bricks from John Matson in Throsk at £12 is particularly interesting as the Matsons were amongst the seventeenth-century potters at Throsk and this may represent a new direction for the pottery which is not mentioned after this date.[8] Metal items came to £98, all for nails and iron bars for windows. Timber was again a major cost at £592 with some extra costs for transport. Dollar was again the main mason, taking £201 for himself and his servants. John Christie, the wright, charged only £43 for himself and his servants and the skailer was paid £110 for roofing. These and other minor costs for clearing up etc. brought the expenditure for the outbuildings to £2,279 and the total expenditure for the scheme to £17,695 (Scots) or £1,475 (Sterling).

After its sale in 1741 the house disappears from the public records. It is mentioned in various nineteenth-century books as Provost Forman's house and shop. By 1921 plans were afoot to demolish the house, along with others in the area. Alternative plans for a restoration of the buildings were drawn up and representations received by the Town Council from the Office of Works, the Commissioners for Ancient Monuments and Sir D. Y. Cameron, saying that their destruction would be 'nothing short of a disaster for the Ancient Royal Burgh of Stirling'. Renovation would have provided more houses than the council's original plans but, since it cost somewhat more, the Housing Committee recommended demolition on 23 February 1925 and the Toun's New House was demolished.[9]

The proponents of the scheme clearly got the fashionable building which they envisaged in asking Smith and McGill to submit designs. From its elegantly arched central doorway to the stylish chimneys, there is nothing vernacular about it. Yet the final decisions on decorative details were actually taken by the council and the whole was executed by local workmen. Particularly significant is the demand for the wild flourish of a 'tympan' followed by sober, technical advice against. A taste for the modern could be dismissed as an isolated civic folly but the availability of the practical skills indicates a steady demand. In the same way, whilst the abandonment of barrel vaulting and the adoption of the platt and scale stair may have been the architects' idea, they must have been confident of the competence of local artisans to carry out their plans.

In this context, the widening of Stirling's building-skills base is noteworthy and the case of painter-plasterers has already been discussed. There was probably only one glazier in Stirling in 1600, increased to about four by 1720. In 1610 the Town Council made enquiries in Glasgow and Dumbarton for a slater able to roof the church and almshouse; on 16 June 1618 Alexander Jack, slater, was admitted as a burgess and thereafter more and more local slaters are recorded.[10] And, as this development shows, Stirling artisans were also learning new techniques, such as how to make sash windows.

The supply of building materials was also being modernised. When Cowane's Hospital was built in the 1630s and 1640s, almost every item of timber had to be bought from afar, some of it specially ordered from Norway and floated up river from Alloa under the personal supervision of the Master of Works. By the late-seventeenth century the Watsons kept a stock of varying specifications, sufficient to supply almost all the demand for such a large project as this. Lime, too, was often bought from a dealer by this time, though sometimes still direct from the quarry.

But there was no firm of 'builders' who would take overall charge, purchase the materials, employ the artisans and deliver a finished building. Materials were bought by the customer who had to co-ordinate the whole effort. It was for the 'pains' of this supervision that the Treasurer was paid £144 (Scots), a sum he surely earned.

This early 'council house' was undeniably a financial disaster. Even if that can be partly excused by a more general collapse in property prices most of the blame must lie with exorbitant building costs. But not all was loss. The house did provide an opportunity for local artisans to demonstrate their skills, it provided a model of good housing for others to follow, it was certainly 'an ornament' and, surely, a boost to civic pride. Its destruction was a far greater folly than its building.

ACKNOWLEDGEMENTS

I am very grateful to Geoffrey Stell for his encouragement to write this paper as well as for several suggestions and improvements and for his invaluable comments on an early draft. My thanks are also due to Dr Rab Houston. All faults are my own.

NOTES

1. Central Region Archives [CRA] Stirling Council Record, B66/20/7 and B66/20/8 record relevant decisions between 8 November 1718 and 20 December 1720; some of this material is re-printed in Renwick, R. (ed.), *Extracts from the Records of the Royal Burgh of Stirling*, vol. 2, 1667–1752, Glasgow, 1889. CRA Burgh Treasurers' Accounts B66/23/1 and B66/21/2 Accounts from 1718 to 1722 record financial details. These two sources are cited without further reference. Dr Rab Houston tells me that the Calton Incorporated Trades owned a tenement combining rented houses and a meeting hall.

2. *Extracts*, vol. 2, p. 97, 21 March 1702; ibid., p. 157–8, 6 December 1718; ibid., p. 183, 1 August 1724; ibid., p. 222, 9 September 1732.

3. H. Colvin, *A Biographical Dictionary of British Architects 1600–1840*, London, 1978; *Extracts*, vol. 2, p. 122, 25 March 1710; ibid., p. 188, 30 April 1726; CRA, Stirling Honorary Burgess Roll, SB1/10/13, 26 July 1709 and 14 September 1709; Charles B. Boog Watson, 'Notes on the names of the closes and wynds of old Edinburgh', *Book of the Old Edinburgh Club*, vol. 12, 1923, pp. 1–156 ('Paisley's Close', p. 44).

4. CRA, Burgh Treasurer's Accounts, B66/23/1, 1722–3, includes an 'Inventar of the arms, drums, worklooms and others ...' with details of fixtures belonging to the town in the houses, stables etc.

5. H. J. Louw, 'The origin of the sash window', *Architectural History*, vol. 26, 1983, pp. 49–72.

6. J. S. Fleming, *Ancient Castles and Mansions of the Stirling Nobility*, Stirling, 1902, pp. 172–3; *Extracts*, vol. 2, pp. 212–13.

7. J. G. Harrison, 'Lime supply in the Stirling area from the 14th to the 18th centuries', *Forth Naturalist and Historian*, vol. 16, pp. 82–9.

8. D. H. Caldwell, V. E. Dean et al., 'The pottery industry at Throsk, Stirlingshire, in the 17th and early 18th century', *Post-Medieval Archaeology*, vol. 26, 1992, pp. 1–46.

9. CRA Stirling Town Council Minutes SB1/1/31, 26 March 1923; SB1/1/32, 27 October 1924; SB1/1/33, 29 December 1924 and 23 February 1925; National Monument Record of Scotland plans STD/143/5–8.

10. *Extracts*, vol. 1, p. 125, 30 July 1610; J. G. Harrison, *Stirling Burgess List 1600–1699*, Stirling, 1991.

JOHN FREW

Concrete, Cosmopolitanism and Low-cost House Design:
The Short Architectural Career of A. H. Campbell, 1923–1926

Focus is brought to bear on the architectural output of Adam Horsburgh
Campbell (1862–1947), Edinburgh Burgh Engineer from 1910 to 1926.
Appointed Director of Housing in 1920, Campbell played a key role in the
formative years of the City's inter-war house building programme, assuming full
architectural responsibility for the Lochend scheme (1923–5), the first of
Edinburgh's large-scale municipal estates to be aimed at the needs of former slum
dwellers. It will be suggested that Campbell's rise to architectural prominence
was achieved at the expense of the City Architect, James A. Williamson, and
attention will also be drawn to his pioneering interest in concrete construction
and the importance of first hand contact with 'advanced' experiments in low cost
housing in the Netherlands.

CAMPBELL WAS FIFTY when he accepted the post of Edinburgh
Burgh Engineer on 5 December 1910.[1] He must have appeared a safe and, at the very least,
uncontroversial appointment, having commenced his career as an assistant in the same office,
remaining for seven years (1882–9) before taking up the first of a succession of municipal
engineering positions south of the border, including posts with Stratford-on-Avon and East
Ham.[2] His work for these latter corporations extended to include architectural responsibilities, the nature of which is suggested by his detailed knowledge of the costs involved in
the provision of artisan dwellings in East London, outlined in evidence supplied to the Royal
Commissioners appointed (1912) to investigate the state of Scottish working class housing.[3]

There was nothing, of course, out of the ordinary in this arrangement, which probably
operated in the majority of late nineteenth-century municipalities, to the extent that the
provision of designs for working class houses was identified as a standard element of the sur-
veyor's brief by Bulnois in his Municipal Engineer's *Handbook* of 1921.[4] Hardly surprisingly,
however, this assumption was resisted at all levels of the architectural profession, which must
have found comfort in the lines of demarcation drawn by Edinburgh Town Council. These
identified the supply of designs for Corporation properties as the specialism of the Super-
intendent of Public works, a long established, if slightly junior, municipal office (redesignated
City Architect in 1919), then held by Campbell's almost exact contemporary, James A.
Williamson.[5]

Vitally, however, Campbell's duties as Burgh Engineer embraced town planning, a still
imprecisely defined area of responsibility that took on added significance later in the decade
when it guaranteed his involvement in the Corporation's preparations for state subsidised

house building, triggered by the mass of communications emanating from the Local Government Board that would eventually coalesce in the requirements of the 1919 Housing and Town Planning Act. Accordingly, it was Campbell, and not Williamson, who attended, in an advisory capacity, the monthly meetings of the newly established Housing and Town Planning Committee, reporting, for example, on potential sites for house building and the number, size and type of house to be adopted under the provisions of the 1919 Act.

His appointment as the Corporation's first ever Director of Housing followed in January 1920.[6] Although denounced by Robert Rowand Anderson ('an Architect [is] the proper person for such a post ... objection should be taken'),[7] the post can be seen to have consolidated an already well established role, albeit one that was at first conceived of in broad administrative terms, co-ordinating the activities of the different architectural firms assigned creative responsibility for the first of the post War housing schemes. The addition of a rider, that the Director of Housing 'shall not ... interfere with such architects in the carrying out of their designs',[8] suggests, however, that the Corporation authorities were well aware of Campbell's wider architectural ambitions, and that it was prepared to resist these at this stage, conceivably out of respect for Williamson, who was responsible for one of the three developments completed under the 1919 Act, the outstanding Gorgie estate.[9]

Whatever the basis for the arrangement, it was undermined by Campbell who, within three years of taking on the duties of Director of Housing, was 'working as an Architect' in a succession of Corporation undertakings. It would later be conceded that this extension of his working brief had never received formal ratification, and that it had 'crept in gradually', exploiting opportunities provided by the Grassmarket and Cowgate Improvement Act (1919).[10] Campbell's initial contribution in this respect again derived from his town planning responsibilities, which involved him in the compilation of a list of substandard properties, and required him to submit recommendations concerning the treatment of buildings of historic and/or exceptional architectural importance (a potentially explosive issue, effectively defused by his advice that the Corporation should seek specialist architectural assistance) as well as provide plans for the rehabilitation of 'non controversial' buildings.[11] His response to this latter obligation reveals him in an insistently pragmatic light, as unexpectedly tolerant of one apartment dwellings (a level of accommodation that fell well below the minimum standards permitted under the 1919 Act) but otherwise content to operate in accordance with guidelines contained in the 1917 Royal Commission Report on the *Housing of the Industrial Population of Scotland*. In the interests of economy, this had encouraged local authorities to make maximum use of existing structures when these were 'externally substantial' although 'internally ... unsatisfactory',[12] advice put into operation (1922) at, for instance, McConnachie's Close in the Cowgate, where the walls of a double tenement were consolidated, the number of internal units reduced and, in the interests of health and hygiene, all rear projections demolished.[13]

3.1 Three-storey tenements, St Clair Street, Leith, 1923–4. (Author)

Plans for entirely new houses followed, at first for three-storey tenemented blocks in the St Clair Street (1923–4) and Sheriff Brae (1924) areas in Leith[14] (Figure 3.1). Although tenements had figured in two of the first phase estates (Abercorn and Wardie), the provision of exclusively tenemented accommodation pointed to a significant shift in Corporation policy, paralleled elsewhere in Scotland as successive local authorities confronted the challenge posed by slum clearances, and the problem of rehousing the poorest sectors of the urban population. As part of the same process the average number of rooms per dwelling was reduced to a two and three (as opposed to three, four and five) apartment mix, contributing to a determined push to reduce building costs, also reflected in a progressive elimination of overtly 'architectural' features, producing, in the case of the St Clair Street tenements, an average costing of £370 per dwelling, less than a third of the price of the houses completed in the immediate aftermath of the 1919 Housing Act.[15]

Remarkably, given the hostility that had surrounded Campbell's appointment as Director of Housing, but perhaps reflecting the relatively modest scale of the St Clair Street and Sheriff Brae developments (66 and 18 houses respectively) this assumption of architectural responsibilities passed without public comment. Compliance within the Council seems to have

3.2 Three-storey tenements, Lochend Quadrant, 1924–5. (Author)

been secured by the savings involved, in terms of fees paid to private architectural firms[16] (responsible for five out of six developments initiated between 1919 and 1922), an explanation that still fails to account for the Corporation's apparent reluctance to involve Williamson, whose effective marginalisation from the housing programme was completed when, on 26 July 1923, Campbell submitted comprehensive plans for the Lochend estate, involving the development of over 120 acres of former agricultural land on the City's eastern boundary, eventually bordered by Lochend Road South, Lochend Avenue, Marionville Road and Findlay Avenue, and identified as suitable for the housing requirements of populations displaced by the Cowgate, Grassmarket and (forthcoming) Leith slum clearance schemes.[17]

These early proposals were for 570 dwellings, rather more than half the number eventually provided (1,034) a total that dwarfed the housing provision at Abercorn (286 units), Wardie (360) and Gorgie (278). Predictably, given the targeted population, and reaffirming a trend already identified at St Clair Street and Sheriff Brae, the new houses were planned as two and three apartment flatted units, supplemented in every case by the provision of a bathroom, scullery and internal wc.[18] Although three-storey tenements figured prominently (Figure 3.2), the majority of the houses conformed (Figure 3.3) to a two-storey, four-flats-

3.3 Four-to-a-block duo slab units, Lochend Gardens, 1924–5. (Author)

to-a-block tenement/flat arrangement (ground floor units accessed independently, upper flats by a shared close), standardising an arrangement already experimented with by David McArthy at Longstone (1921–2).[19]

The decision to build the Lochend houses in concrete was taken in September 1923,[20] and followed an inspection of houses in Newcastle and Leeds, erected to the 'duo slab' cavity wall system promoted by William Airey and Sons of Leeds, who, having erected eight specimen four unit blocks along the north side of Marionville Road (1923–4) (Figure 3.4), were eventually assigned the building contract for 607 of the Lochend units, sited to the south of Sleigh Drive.[21] Although concrete had been employed in a significant number of the post War estates, the vast majority of houses thereby erected (as, for instance, at Wardie and those Lochend houses between Sleigh Drive and Lochend Avenue, by the Bo'ness builders John Hardie and Sons) were constructed out of pre-cast blocks, laid in traditional fashion, with external facings frequently moulded in imitation of masonry. In a slight but telling shift of emphasis, the Airey houses incorporated identical pre-cast slabs, interlocking at regular intervals with poured concrete stanchions, a system that not only eliminated waste but was capable of being undertaken by unskilled labour,[22] described as comprising eighty per cent of the Lochend workforce in December 1924.[23]

3.4 Two-storey duo slab units, Marionville Road, Lochend, 1923–4. (Author)

To Corporation gratification, therefore, the estate was pushed through to completion with impressive speed, with the majority of houses declared ready for occupation in October 1925.[24] By this date Campbell's career had taken a further, and unexpected, turn. Already an inveterate attender of Housing and Town Planning conferences, he was invited, in the summer of 1924, to participate in a study tour of Dutch housing, as part of a delegation that included the Liverpool City Engineer John Brodie and the weighty figure of Sir Charles Ruthven, Director General of Housing at the Board of Health.[25] The working party's brief, to 'inquire into new methods of construction',[26] confirms that it was conceived of as part of the cost cutting programme that would culminate in the swingeing economies adopted under the Conservative administration in the mid- and late 1920s, explaining its interest in the sometimes drastic economics effected by the Amsterdam and Hague authorities, revealed, for example, by the elimination of hallways and corridors and, in houses where gas cookers were provided in the kitchen, open fireplaces.[27] Importantly, special attention was paid to advances in concrete construction,[28] an area of interest that presumably explains Campbell's presence in the party, and which led it to focus, in particular, on the supposed advantages of the Korrelbeton system, adopted in the Amsterdam Ooster Park and Betendorp developments:

> The distinctive feature of the construction is that the material is run in semi-
> liquid form into prepared moulds or shuttering. It very quickly hardens, and
> the result is a wall some eight inches thick, of great strength but semi-porous.
> The material consists of clinker, or the ash-like refuse of destructors, mixed
> with cement. The house is made practically in one piece. In practice, the walls
> at one operation are carried up to the height of the first storey. The next storey
> is added later. A thin coating of plaster is given to the walls, outside and
> inside.[29]

The end result was identified as lightweight and rigid (permitting potential savings in the
provision of foundations), as well as wind, water, sound and vermin proof. Equally importantly, and to an even greater extent than the 'duo slab' system, it circumvented skilled brick-
laying methods, evidenced by the observation that the Betendorp houses had been erected
by a workforce composed of market gardeners, cigar makers and diamond workers.[30]

The delegation report was never published, explaining Campbell's decision to circulate
his own version of its findings to interested local authorities, under the title 'Houses in
Holland'.[31] Further evidence of his enthusiasm for the Dutch achievement was provided by
developments at Lochend, by the introduction, in three-storey tenements, of rear access
balconies[32] (a more or less standard element of Dutch tenement design,[33] that had been
studiously avoided in the first of the British post War estates) and, almost inevitably, a belated
flirtation with the Korrelbeton system, in the form of 52 four-unit blocks (some with flat
roofs), erected (1925–6) to his specifications by the Corolite Construction Limited, center-
ing on Restalrig Square and Restalrig Circus (Figure 3.5).[34]

A description of Campbell at the very end of his career claims that he was working sixteen-
hours a day,[35] attending to a multiplicity of duties that included, in his last year of office, the
drawing up of plans for the Prestonfield and Saughtonhall estates,[36] the submission of
recommendations in support of five hundred prefabricated 'steel' houses in the Lochend,
Abercorn, Easter Road and Wardie areas,[37] and attendance at at least three Housing and
Town Planning conferences.[38] His retirement, on 3 June 1926, was followed by an acri-
monious debate within the Council, reflected in the decision ('by a small majority') to reject the proposal that he be awarded an additional gratuity for the architectural work he had
undertaken during his period as Director of Housing,[39] an outcome that was undoubtedly
influenced by a near complete breakdown in relations with the City Architect's Department.[40] The actions subsequently taken by Williamson's successor as City Architect,
Ebenezer MacRae, point, indeed, to a conscious settling of old scores, revealed by his
decision to accept the duties, but dispense with the title, of Director of Housing, and to
transfer the sizeable architectural staff Campbell had recruited from the Burgh Engineer's
to the City Architect's office, effectively eliminating all trace of what had come to assume
the significance of a rival establishment.[41]

Campbell's legacy was nevertheless considerable. In particular, he can be identified as
having assumed a pioneering role in the promotion of concrete as a solution to low cost

3.5 Korrelbeton houses, by Corrolite Construction Ltd, Restalrig Square, 1925–6. (Author)

national housing requirements, and to have consolidated a format (i.e. the two-storey Lochend formula) that would gain widespread application in the 1920s and 1930s, locally and nationally.[42] In addition, it is surely not unreasonable to identify Campbell as a significant link in the chain of municipal cosmopolitanism, a tradition that would assume unusual importance in the 1930s, finding a particularly forceful exponent in MacRae, whose own major Continental study tour (1934) commenced in the Netherlands,[43] testifying to a lasting (if unacknowledged) debt to the events of the preceding decade.

University of St Andrews

NOTES

1. *Edinburgh Town Council Minutes (ETCM)*, 1925/6, pp. 367–9.

2. Ibid.; *The Evening Dispatch*, 7 January 1947; *The Scotsman*, 7 January 1947, p. 3.

3. *The Evening Dispatch*, 7 January 1947; *Report of the Royal Commission on the Housing of the Industrial Population of Scotland Rural and Urban*, Edinburgh, 1917, p. 68.

4. H. P. Boulnois, *Municipal Engineering: Surveying the Scope of Municipal*

Engineering and the Statutory Position, The Appointment, the Training, and the Duties of a Municipal Engineer, London, 1921, pp. 47, 72, 85.

5. It was therefore Williamson who assumed full responsibility for the designs of Portobello Town Hall (1909–12), the largest Edinburgh Corporation undertaking in the years immediately preceding the Great War.

6. *ETCM*, 1918/19, pp. 532–4; 1919/20, p. 81; 1925/6, p. 368.

7. *Minute Book, Institute of Scottish Architects*, vol. 1, p. 84.

8. *ETCM*, 1918/19, pp. 532–4.

9. For this, and the other first-phase estates, see J. Frew, 'Homes Fit for Heroes: Early Municipal House Building in Edinburgh', *Journal of the Architectural Heritage Society of Scotland*, 1989, no. 16, pp. 26–33.

10. *ETCM*, 1925/6, p. 368.

11. *ETCM*, 1918/19, pp. 532–4; 1920/1, p. 611; 1921/2, pp. 223–5, 886–96; *Minutes of the Housing and Town Planning Committee*, 1920/1, pp. 138, 147; 1921/2, pp. 18–20, 149–154, 156; 1922/3, pp. 81, 139.

12. *ETCM*, 1922/3, p. 26; Royal Commission *Report*, pp. 315–16.

13. *Minutes of the Housing and Town Planning Committee*, 1921/22, p. 40. Campbell's observations on the Scottish 'tenemented' tradition are summarised in Royal Commission *Report*, p. 49.

14. *ETCM*, 1922/3, p. 693; 1925/6, p. 369. The Sheriff Brae block was demolished in *c*.1990.

15. *ETCM*, 1924/5, pp. 135–7.

16. *ETCM*, 1925/6, pp. 368–9.

17. *ETCM*, 1922/3, p. 776.

18. Ibid.

19. Frew, 'Homes Fit for Heroes', pp. 31–2.

20. *ETCM*, 1922/3, pp. 867, 890; *The Scotsman*, 10 October 1923, pp. 8, 12.

21. *ETCM*, 1923/4, pp. 570–1.

22. *ETCM*, 1923/4, pp. 570–1, 663. *The Scotsman*, 7 January 1923, p. 8; 5 December 1924, p. 5. A. Christie, *A Guide to Non-Traditional Housing in Scotland 1923–55*, Edinburgh, 1987, pp. 4, 43–4.

23. Ibid.

24. *ETCM*, 1924/5, p. 477.

25. *The Scotsman*, 2 December 1924, p. 7.

26. Ibid.

27. Ibid.

28. Ibid.

29. Ibid., 2 December 1924, p. 7; 5 December 1924, pp. 5–6.

30. Ibid.

31. See e.g. *Dundee Town Council Minutes*, 1923/4, p. 1242.

32. *ETCM*, 1924/5, p. 690. These features were replaced in the 1980s.

33. 'An almost standard feature', commented on in *The Scotsman*, 5 December, 1924, p. 6.

34. *ETCM*, 1924/5, p. 140; 1926/7, p. 775. Christie, *Non-Traditional Housing*, pp. 40–2.

35. *The Scotsman*, 7 January 1947, p. 3.

36. *ETCM*, 1924/5, pp. 113–14; 1925/6, pp. 439, 495, 680, 735.

37. *ETCM*, 1924/5, pp. 737–8; 1925/6, p. 445.

38. *ETCM*, 1924/5, pp. 206, 604.

39. *ETCM*, 1925/6, pp. 368–9; *The Scotsman*, 7 January 1947, p. 3.

40. Confirmed by Mr Duncan Ogilvie, who commenced work as a clerical assistant in the City Architect's Department in 1923. Interviewed, 4 October 1990.

41 *ETCM*, 1925/6, pp. 475–7, 566–7.

42. Experimented with, e.g. by James Brown in the Dundee Mid-Craigie development (1935–6). For other examples (in Edinburgh and Aberdeen), see the Department of Health for Scotland, *Housing of the Working Classes – Scotland: Economically Planned Houses of Satisfactory Design*, Edinburgh, 1933, pp. 11, 23.

43. MacRae's Continental study tours are investigated in J. Frew, 'Ebenezer MacRae and Reformed Tenement Design', *St Andrews Studies in the History of Scottish Architecture and Design*, vol. 2, 1991, pp. 80–7.

ANTHONY LEWIS WITH JOHN LOWREY

James Craig: Architect of the First New Town of Edinburgh

James Craig (1744–95) is best known as the designer of Edinburgh's first New Town, but recently considerable doubt has been cast on his claim to its author-ship. This paper reappraises the evidence and concludes that the original attribution is sound.

JAMES CRAIG'S CONTRIBUTION to Scottish urban design marks him out as one of the most important architects of his time. Not only did he design Edinburgh's first New Town, but he was almost certainly the 'Mr Craig architect in Edinburgh' who was employed to lay out much of central Glasgow's grid of streets, giving him the distinction of shaping the character of Scotland's two most important cities.[1] In addition, he designed streets, circuses, squares, churches, gardens, monuments, bridges, a crescent and an octagon for Edinburgh, and worked as an architect elsewhere. These designs, and his published essay, *Plan for Improving the City of Edinburgh* (1786), clearly show that Craig was aware of modern theories and practice relating to the planning of towns.

On 3 June 1767 Craig received an inscribed gold medal and silver box containing the freedom of the city as the prizes for his success in the New Town competition. This achievement became the cornerstone of his future career and the New Town design remains by far his best-known work.[2] Craig exploited his new found fame and developed his reputation by publishing the plan in 1768 (Figure 4.1). In 1788, he celebrated his plan further by striking a commemorative medal that was placed in the foundation of his monument to George Buchanan.[3]

The New Town has been so important, not only to Craig's career but also to our subsequent appraisal of his work, that there can be little doubt that there would be no bicentenary celebrations in 1995 were it not for his involvement in its design; and yet doubt has been cast on his authorship of the plan as it was published and executed. Stuart Harris has suggested that William Mylne, not James Craig, should receive most of the credit for the design of the first New Town.[4] His argument is based on important archival research, and develops ideas put forward by Dr D. Simpson (1967)[5] and M. K. Meade (1971).[6] These two earlier papers suggest that one of two maps of Midlothian, made by John Laurie in 1766,[7] showing 'New Edinburgh' on the site of the New Town (Figure 4.2), provide clues to the nature of Craig's prize-winning design and to the genesis of the plan as finally executed. Harris accepts this and, using the minutes of the North Bridge Committee, arrives at the Mylne attribution. Craig emerges from this as an inexperienced and naive designer who won the competition but did not see his vision realised. It is the purpose of this paper to

4.1 James Craig, engraved plan of the New Town, 1768. (National Library of Scotland)

re-examine this question and to consider the strength of the arguments presented by Mr Harris.

The competition to design the New Town was advertised in the *Caledonian Mercury*, on 22 March 1766. John Laurie had prepared a survey plan of the area of the proposed New Town, on behalf of the Town Council and for the use of the competition entrants who were to lay out 'regular streets and buildings to be built'.[8] The rewards for winning the competition were advertised on 9 April in the Edinburgh press.[9] Two days later a fuller advertisement for architects to make plans was published.[10] This time the streets had to have a 'proper breadth', include by-lanes, and the New Town was to have a reservoir and any public buildings required. The finished plans had to be sent to the Lord Provost under sealed covers, with the architects' names on separate, sealed pieces of paper. Only the winning name was to be revealed.

On 2 August 1766, John Laurie advertised his map for sale in the *Caledonian Mercury* and it was duly published two days later.[11] This was the very day on which Commissioner George Clerk and John Adam identified plan number 4 (Craig's plan) as 'the best of those we have seen'[12] and a full twenty-two days before the North Bridge Committee, which was the final judge of the competition, chose the same plan and made the result public. This presents a problem for anyone who wishes to identify Laurie's plan with Craig's competition winning design. Harris notes the disparity in dates but contends that Laurie 'evidently' was privy to this important information.[13] There is, however, no solid evidence of any kind to support such a contention and the attribution of Laurie's first plan to Craig is therefore immediately suspect. However, Harris's argument does not depend on this and where he goes beyond Simpson and Meade is in his interpretation of the second Laurie plan, published later in 1766, and in his use of two very important pieces of documentary evidence from the minutes of the North Bridge Committee.

The first of these is the record of Craig's success in the competition:

> The Committee having taken into consideration the different Plans given into them in consequence of the advertisements, and having taken the opinion of George Clerk and John Adams Esquaires thereon are unanimously of the opinion that the Plan (no 4) has the most merit and that the author of it is entitled to the Premium of a Gold Medal with the Impression of the arms of the city of Edinburgh and the freedom of the city in a silver box, the value of the said medal and box being twenty five guineas, or if he shall incline that he shall receive the said sum in money with the freedom of the city, though they do not find that the said Plan has so much merit as to be adopted as the Plan to be carried into Execution and that it may be of use giving others hints to improve upon. And having opened the private mark of the said Plan (no 4) they find the name 'James Craig' contained therein as the author's name.[14]

Clearly, the prize-winning design was not simply to be carried forward into execution, and clearly other people were to become involved in the design process. There is even a hint that Craig himself would be superseded.

4.2 John Laurie, map of Midlothian, showing 'New Edinburgh', 1766. (National Library of Scotland)

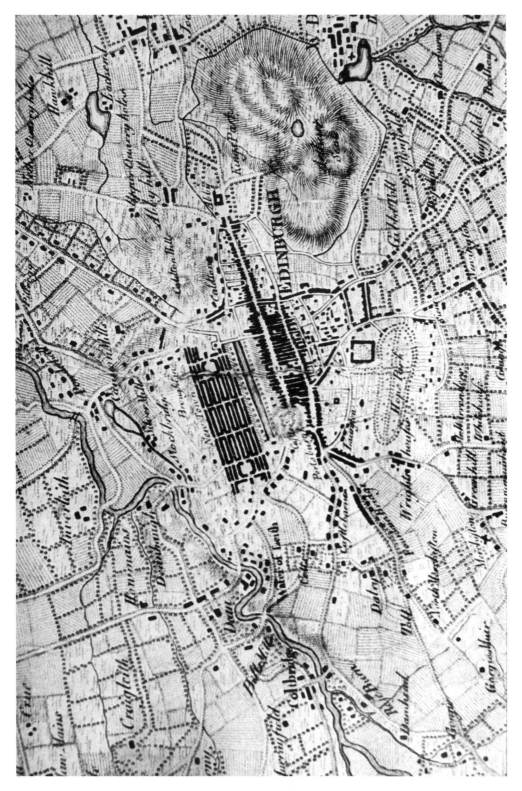

4.3 John Laurie, map of Midlothian, showing Edinburgh's 'New Town', 1766. (National Library of Scotland)

A second piece of documentary evidence is dated 22 October 1766, when William Mylne is recorded as making out 'the Plan of the New Town and Improvements on the North of the City.'[15] By 29 October he had completed his plan and 'the rectified Plan of the improvements made out by William Mylne mason was laid before the Committee and the New Town Plan Committee on which sat Lord Kaimes, Sir James Clerk, Commissioner Clerk and Mr John Adam to examine.'[16] This, so the thesis runs, is evidence of Mylne's re-working of the prize-winning design by the young and inexperienced Craig. It is identified with a re-issue of Laurie's map showing a second version of the New Town design (Figure 4.3), and since it contains the fundamentals of the final New Town design, the re-attribution to Mylne is justified. Any other plans produced between this time and the final approval of the plan in July 1767, are interpreted as variations on Mylne's basic, gridded theme.

One of the most interesting and unusual aspects of this thesis is that this interpretation of the documentary evidence is secondary to the interpretation of the two versions of the New Town plans published by Laurie. The reattribution to Mylne depends fundamentally on a particular reading of those plans and their integration with the documentary evidence already outlined. Harris argues that although the two plans are different, they are clearly related 'and as clearly the second is a more masterly reworking of the first.'[17] Having established this, and having established that the second Laurie plan represents Mylne's 'rectified plan', it is then possible to argue that the first Laurie plan is Craig's competition entry. The grounds for this are that since Mylne was called on to rectify Craig and since the grid, identified as the Mylne plan, is a 'masterly reworking' of the first, then the first plan must be Craig's. As back up to this theory, we are offered the wording of the Bridge Committee minutes when Craig's success in the competition was recorded but the impracticality of his design noted. Since the design shown on Laurie's plan is somewhat impractical, the two must be linked.

This somewhat circular and self-referential line of argument is open to a number of objections but the most important one is that the link, based on Harris's visual analysis, between the two plans illustrated by Laurie is simply not established as fact, and Harris's entire thesis depends on that link being accepted. The two plans are quite different and although there are some similarities it is much easier to explain those in terms of the shape and topography of the site than one plan representing remedial action on the other. Another major problem is that, although there is an argument to establish Craig as the designer of the first of the Laurie plans, no argument is provided in favour of the Mylne attribution.[18] Furthermore, there is no reason to link Mylne's plan with Laurie's second plan. All we know of that plan is that it was produced later in the year than the first one, we do not know that it was produced at or around the time Mylne's plan was finished. (And even if it did, it would not prove any connection between the two plans.) Since Craig was also working on plans at around the same time as Mylne (discussed below), we might just as easily suggest that Laurie's second plan represents Craig's thoughts on the matter. All we can say for certain about Mylne is that he was clearly involved in some capacity in the evolution of the final design of the New Town but that is a very different matter from re-attributing the design to him.

The purpose of Laurie's map was to illustrate the arable and pasture grounds in and around Edinburgh. It was partly inspired, so he claimed, by similar maps of London and Paris (possibly one reason why the title of the map is given in French as well as English).[19] Laurie was certainly well aware of what, in general, was proposed for the site beyond the Nor' Loch and his additions to the map might easily be explained by his own speculations as to what form the new development would take. Neither 'design' responds well to the actual site and it could easily be the case that Laurie was simply offering a couple of possibilities, as an indication of, and publicity for, what was to follow. Interestingly, there are some parallels between Laurie's two versions of the New Town and the work of John Gwynn, whose book, *City of London and Westminster Improved*, published in June 1766,[20] advocated grids of streets, and contains a design of a square with streets radiating from it.[21]

So far, we have discussed four main pieces of evidence, two visual and two documentary, and we have argued that the links between them are too weak to admit of any re-attribution of the New Town design. There is further evidence, both negative and positive, which is strong enough to suggest that William Mylne is not the designer and that James Craig almost certainly is.

First let us consider the additional evidence against the Mylne attribution. William Mylne was a professional mason and architect who did a lot of work for the city and was already contracted to build the North Bridge by 1766. Payments for his work can be traced in Edinburgh Town Council accounts. If he had been requested to undertake so large a task as the design of the New Town, we would surely expect this to show up in the council's accounts. There is no such account and no such payment was made. On the other hand, Mylne did present the council with an account for making improvements around the north bridge by setting up a dyke and ditch in the south-eastern corner of Barefoot's Parks (the area on which the New Town was to be built) on 28 October 1766; the day before he presented his plan of improvements to the North Bridge Committee. It is possible, therefore, that the references to that plan in fact refer to this very limited work and not to the design of the New Town as a whole.[22]

A second piece of evidence against the Mylne attribution is the deafening silence from the Mylne papers on this subject. Robert Mylne, William's elder brother, kept the family papers and used them to write a history of the Mylne family and their considerable achievements.[23] The New Town competition was certainly a big enough project to include in this and had William played any significant role in the design of the New Town there can be little doubt that it would have been included. However, there is no such reference, rather, in the opening pages there is the interesting snippet of information that 'the design for a New Town by James Craig was approved'.[24]

With that we turn to the positive evidence in favour of Craig, and having the official spokesman for the alternative attribution on his side is quite a good start. However, there is more than this. On 10 December 1766 the minutes of the North Bridge Committtee record that 'there was produced two Plans in different views, made out by Mr James Craig, of the proposed Improvements, with a plan of common shores [sewers], which was remitted to the same committee, to whom Convener Mylne's plan was remitted'.[25]

The same difficulties that beset the interpretation of the minutes dealing with Mylne's contribution, apply here also. The plans are lost and there is little documentary evidence to cast light on their appearance. What is quite clear though, is that both Mylne and Craig produced plans of some kind and there is no reason to give Mylne's contribution greater prominence than Craig's. Harris argues that Craig's plans 'in different views' were in support of Mylne's overall plan and that the 'different views' refer to elevations of houses, on the one hand, and sections through streets (to show the sewers) on the other.[26] This fits in neatly with the idea that Craig was acting in some subordinate capacity to Mylne but it is not supported by the evidence and the explanation offered by Harris is thoroughly unconvincing. At this stage of the New Town project house elevations were not the concern of the planners and there was simply no reason for Craig to consider the design of elevations. Similarly, the idea that Craig was drawing sections through the streets of the New Town is not only unsupported by any evidence, but would also have been a highly unusual method of presentation in Britain at that time and would have linked Craig with the most advanced French town-planning theory.[27]

Whatever Craig's two plans 'in different views' looked like, one thing is perfectly clear: he was deeply involved in the amendment of his competition plan to make it suitable for execution.[28] In 1767, the council, and its various committees, vigorously pursued their objective of having the Extension Bill pushed through Parliament. This involved the expertise of men like Craig, Laurie, and Mylne on many occasions but it becomes quite clear that Craig was the major figure and was recognised as the designer of the proposed New Town. For example, council minutes for 24 June 1767 show that Lord Kaimes, Lord Alemore and Commissioner Clerk, 'and other persons of skill in these matters had reviewed all the former plans with the greatest care and attention, and considered several amendments proposed by Mr Craig, and that Mr Craig, by their direction, had made out a new plan, which plan, signed by the Lord Provost was produced.'[29] The council minutes for 29 July contain a very similar entry, stating that a committee appointed to prepare the plan for the extended Royalty 'considered amendments proposed by Mr Craig, who, on their instructions, has made out a new plan, now produced, signed by the Lord Provost.'[30]

Finally, Craig's involvement did not end with the approval of his plan on 29 July 1767. He continued to work on the practicalities of realising the dream of the New Town, for example in the production of feuing plans.[31] He also retained his interest in the sewers and in October 1767 volunteered to go to London to learn more about these essential amenities.[32] It is not all clear what Craig learned about sewers on this trip but it is quite certain that it was to prove important both for the final plan of the New Town and for Craig's subsequent career. The immediate result was that the plan was changed again. A letter from Sir John Pringle to the Council states that the plan 'was drawn upon by some well wishers not only of the young architect but of the design in general', and that some of the street names had been changed: the King himself changing St Giles Street to Princes Street and naming Frederick Street.[33]

However, the most important news Pringle had to give was that the inscription that the council had wanted to give its plan had arrived too late to receive royal approval, and, in its absence, Craig had dedicated the plan to the King himself, with the consent of the royal Masters of Buildings and those 'nearest the King's person'. It has been suggested that Craig incurred the council's displeasure for missing them out of the dedication[34] but there is no evidence for this and Craig continued to enjoy the council's patronage on his return to Edinburgh in 1768. From that point on, his career entered its most successful phase as he cashed in on his success in the New Town project. This success was partly based on the highly impressive engraved plan he published in the Spring of 1768 (Figure 4.1), and it is this plan that provides us with a final, and crucial, piece of evidence of Craig's authorship of the design. The engraving (and indeed the ms. plan on which it is based) bears the inscription 'Ja. Craig Arch. inven. et delin.' This is a quite explicit statement of authorship that cannot simply be ignored. It means that James Craig was either the designer of the New Town or he was a liar. The latter is highly unlikely, since such inscriptions on prints are generally an excellent guide to authorship. If Craig had lied it is inconceivable that someone would not have objected, and probably very vehemently and litigiously. It is incumbent, therefore, on any scholar who wishes to deny Craig's authorship of the New Town plan to prove that this inscription is wrong, and until that is done, Craig's role remains secure.[35]

This does not, of course mean that the plan that won the competition is the plan that was engraved in 1768 or that Craig was free to amend his plan without the advice and ideas of others. The whole committee structure involved in the approval of the plan makes it quite clear that a number of people, including William Mylne, John Adam, Lord Kaimes, and various other 'persons of skill', were involved in the development of the plan. However, it is equally clear that Craig played the most important role in this development; his is the name that occurs most frequently in all kinds of official records, his is the name that appears on the final plan and he is the man who should remain securely credited as designer of the first New Town.

ACKNOWLEDGEMENTS
Anthony Lewis is grateful for the considerable assistance of the staff at Edinburgh City Archive; Edinburgh City Library, Edinburgh Room and at the National Library of Scotland, Manuscript department. Dr Nicholas Philipson also provided advice and encouragement which is gratefully acknowledged.

NOTES

1. Strathclyde Regional Archives, C.1.1.40., Council Act Book, November 1791–October 1793, vol. 35, p. 173.

2. The other important element in Craig's success was his kinship to James Thomson, the popular poet, who was his uncle. The importance of Thomson to Craig cannot be discussed in depth here, but Thomson's poetry does figure in Craig's work from time to time, most notably on the New Town plan. His exploitation of this relationship was commented upon unfavourably in his obituary in the *Scots Register*, vol. 6, 1796, pp. 361–2.

3. Edinburgh University Library, Special Collections, Df.2.51.

4. Stuart Harris, 'New Light on the First New Town', *Book of the Old Edinburgh Club*, New Series, vol. 2, 1992, pp. 1–13.

5. D. C. Simpson, 'City Plans and the New Town', *University of Edinburgh Journal*, vol. 23, 1967, pp. 52–7.

6. M. K. Meade, 'Plans of the New Town of Edinburgh', *Architectural History*, vol. 14, 1971, pp. 41–4.

7. National Library of Scotland (NLS), EMS.s.36 and EMGB.b.2.1.

8. *Caledonian Mercury*, 22 March 1766.

9. Ibid., 9 April 1766.

10. Ibid., 11 April 1766.

11. Harris, 'New Light on the First New Town', n. 37.

12. Edinburgh City Archives (ECA), Bay D, bundle 125, shelf 9, packet 118.

13. Harris, 'New Light on the First New Town', p. 9.

14. ECA, *Sederunt Book of the Committee appointed by the Town Council of Edinburgh for forwarding the Scheme of Communication with the Fields on the North of the City by a Bridge over the North Loch, 7.11.1764–31.1.1770*, 26 August 1766.

15. Ibid., 22 October 1766.

16. Ibid., 29 October 1766.

17. Harris, 'New Light on the First New Town', p. 5.

18. Ibid., p. 9, states that Laurie's second plan 'showed a representation of Mylne's plan', but the only link seems to be his argument that both plans were in some sense 'rectifications' of something else.

19. *Caledonian Mercury*, 6 August 1766.

20. John Gwynn, *City of London and Westminster Improved*, London, 1766. The Stationers Court Records (NLS) show that this book was published by 13 June 1766.

21. Ibid., p. 6. 'It is to be wished that the ground plans of all great cities and towns were composed of right lines, and that the streets intersected each other at right angles ... indeed, if it was practicable, a square or circular forms should be preferred in all capital cities as best adapted to grandeur and convenience, in the centre of which is a spacious opening where the King's palace should be situated. ... a vast city ought to have at least three capital streets which should have run through the whole, and at convenient distances being intersected by other capital streets at right angles, by which means all

the inferior streets would have an easy and convenient communication with them.'

22. The account is in ECA, *Tradesmens' Accounts, 1752–1767*, p. 501. This interpretation of the evidence is offered slightly tongue in cheek. It may do Mylne a disservice but it is no less plausible than the proposition that he completely redesigned the New Town.

23. Scottish Record Office, RH4/82; *Robert Mylne, Family Scrapbook, 1734–1811*.

24. Ibid.; this appears on the opening page of Mylne's *Scrapbook*.

25. ECA, *Sederunt Book*, 26 August 1766, 10 December 1766.

26. Harris, 'New Light on the First New Town', p. 5.

27. Antoine Picon, *French Architects and Engineers in the Age of Enlightenment*, Cambridge, 1992, pp. 198–9, reproduces an engraving of a section through a street from Pierre Patte's *Mémoires sur les Objets les Plus Importantes de l'Architecture* (1769) and states that it was one of the very first examples of such a view.

28. Andrew Fraser has made the intriguing suggestion that the plans 'in different views' actually refer to alternative treatments of the ground plan, one of which was the famous Circus plan, previously dated to 1774. This view is to be elaborated in a forthcoming article (1995).

29. ECA, *Town Council Minutes*, 24 June 1767.

30. Ibid., 29 July 1767. This entry marks the final, official approval of the New Town plan.

31. Referred to, for example, in *Information for the Lord Provost, Magistrates, Edinburgh Town Council versus John Deas, esq*, 5 March 1773, in ECA, *Pamphlets*.

32. ECA, *Town Council Minutes*, 14 October 1767.

33. ECA, *Town Council Minutes*, 23 December 1767.

34. Meade, 'Plan of the New Town of Edinburgh', pp. 41–4.

35. Harris, 'New Light on the First New Town', n. 40, argues that the inscription on the plan must be wrong because it contradicts his argument. It is interesting that Harris is willing to accept the reliability of such inscriptions when he argues against the attribution of a design for the North Bridge to Craig (n. 11) on the grounds that it bears the word '*delineavit*' and not '*invenit*'. The rigour of that argument does not, however, extend to the New Town plan.

5.1 David Hamilton, Lennox Castle (1837–41), view from north-east, 1954. (RCAHMS)

DIANE WATTERS

David Hamilton's Lennox Castle

Lennox Castle (Figure 5.1) was David Hamilton's only essay in the neo-Romanesque style. This article traces the house's conception and building, setting it in the wider context of Hamilton's oeuvre, and the international trends in neo-Romanesque architecture.

INTRODUCTION

IN THE 1964 REPORT to the Historic Buildings Council, *Castellated and Gothic Houses in Scotland, 1745–1840*, the author claimed that 'Lennox, ugly and ill-proportioned, is a difficult house to evaluate justly'.[1] David Hamilton's (1768–1843) other revivalist works of the 1830s have often been evaluated in a similar way.[2] It is outwith the scope of this article to investigate the changing tastes and critical approaches of architectural historians towards nineteenth-century revivalism. The specific aim of this paper is to re-evaluate Lennox Castle, not only as an important work in Hamilton's career, but as part of the wider development of mid- and late nineteenth-century revivalism in Scotland. This re-appraisal is also fuelled by the fact that Lennox Castle is now under threat. Lennox Castle Mental Defectives' Institution, which was built immediately adjacent to the house after 1927, is scheduled for eventual closure, and there are plans to convert the castle itself into thirty-three dwellings.

This examination will focus on three areas: firstly, the history of the building commission; secondly, a general architectural analysis of the castle; and, finally, a discussion of the particular question of its style. Lennox Castle's conception and building was a major project, in which David Hamilton was involved as early as 1834, and a brief account of this under-lines, among other things, the political motives of the client, and the professional cunning of the architect in gaining the commission. The layout and logic of the main spaces are then examined, with the aid of a recent plan of the principal floor, measured and drawn in 1994 by the Royal Commission on the Ancient and Historical Monuments of Scotland: an analysis of the castle reveals the continuity in Hamilton's own work, and highlights, in particular, the national tradition within which his domestic work developed. Stylistically, the decision to adopt a neo-Romanesque manner has previously been attributed solely to the client,[3] but a brief examination of the international revival of neo-Romanesque architecture in the 1830s and '40s, and of possible Romanesque stylistic sources within Scotland, is used to question this assumption.

HISTORY OF THE BUILDING COMMISSION

In 1833 John Lennox Kincaid Lennox officially succeeded to the estate of Woodhead, near Lennoxtown in Stirlingshire, taking over from his aunt, Margaret Lennox, and becoming the 16th of Balcorrach and 11th of Woodhead.[4] He and his wife, Frances Maxwell, a member of the Cunninghame family of Craigends, inherited a large estate, and an existing mansion: Woodhead House. Woodhead had a late sixteenth-century core, which had been altered several times, most recently in the early nineteenth century.[5] There exists, within the Lennox Estate papers, a set of four drawings, showing two schemes for significantly altering and extending Woodhead.[6] Both schemes are classically inspired, symmetrical, and with castellated features. They are undated, signed 'John Paterson, Edinburgh', and inscribed with the client's name: 'John Lennox Esq.' We may assume that the latter was the 14th of Balcorrach, who died in 1811, and that the architect was John Paterson, one-time assistant to Robert Adam, who died in 1832.

Kincaid Lennox initially pursued his uncle's plans for the extension of Woodhead. John Cameron, historian of Campsie parish, claims that the proprietor employed David Hamilton in 1833, to prepare plans for this purpose, but that Hamilton suggested Woodhead should be abandoned owing to problems of 'site and style'.[7] Plans for Woodhead were supposedly drawn up, but pressure from Lennox's architect and advisors eventually changed his decision, and led him instead to build a new home. This latter claim is supported by a letter of September 1832, from William Bonar, Francis Lennox's brother-in-law, which details a visit to Woodhead, and suggests that he may have encouraged Lennox against his initial plan. He describes the estate and house:

> To the south the hill rises to a very considerable height and is clothed with beautiful plantations of different ages and very judiciously disposed which make a very beautiful termination of the view in front of the house. On the whole it is a property of very great capabilities – tho I fear from the little that is doing or proposed to be done there is not much likelihood of the proper advantage being taken of its localities.[8]

We must here briefly digress from our account of the evolution of the project, to examine in more detail why Lennox eventually decided to build the new Lennox Castle rather than rebuild Woodhead, and how David Hamilton came to be the new house's architect. The 1830s were, of course, a great period of country house building and improvement, and Lennox Castle can be seen as merely another example of this. However, Lennox may have had a more immediate motive for building a new castle, stemming from family politics. As explained above, he had succeeded to the estate after his aunt, Margaret Lennox, had died without issue. Miss Lennox had spent a great deal of time and effort attempting to regain the lapsed title and honours of the ancient Earls of Lennox. She had believed herself to be the rightful living heir to a title, which by the feudal incident of non-entry had fallen into the hands of the sovereign in 1459. That title, of Earl of Lennox, had subsequently existed only as a gift of the crown. In 1813, a book, *The Case of Margaret Lennox of Woodhead, in Relation to the Title, Honours and Dignity of the Ancient Earls of Levenax or Lennox*, was published with her backing: it cleverly set out her claim to the title, using the charters she then had in her possession, and which subsequently passed on to Kincaid Lennox.[9] The book's genealogical table traced her family's line of descent back to Arckill, a Saxon baron who came to Scotland in 1069; his son, Alwyne MacArckill, first Earl of Lennox, was the ultimate ancestor of the Ballcorrach-Woodhead line, from which Margaret herself descended. The opening line reads: 'This family is of high antiquity. It is of Saxon origin.'[10] The exact details of the book's genealogical argumentation are not important to the building of Lennox Castle, but its emotive opening statement reveals Margaret's commitment, and seems likely to have shaped Lennox's approach to his new title, and his new home.

Cameron claims that Lennox and his wife sympathised with Margaret's pursuit, and themselves intended to petition the Government to restore the title, but that, mostly for financial reasons, they abandoned this goal.[11] Thus, the picture is inconclusive: Lennox seems to have been aware of the practical benefits of retaining the existing ancestral family home, and the emotive appeal of building a new grander castle, in his supposed pursuit of the title of Earl.

Although David Hamilton is held by Cameron to have drawn up plans for an extended Woodhead,[12] there is no direct documentation to support this. Hamilton is first mentioned in the Lennox Estate Papers in March 1835, in relation to mason work carried out by a Mr J. Robertson for the stables and offices to be erected at Woodhead.[13] This same Robertson had been contracted, the previous May, in 1834, for two new windows 'proposed upon the north front of Woodhead House'.[14] It seems unlikely, therefore, that Hamilton's involvement at Woodhead extended to anything more significant than the building of the stable and office block. This block is shown, just south-west of the Castle, in the first edition Ordnance Survey map of 1860, and is listed in the notice of sale of the Lennox Castle Estate in 1927; by 1936, however, it had vanished.[15]

But Hamilton may have taken the smaller commission of the stables and offices in the knowledge that his client was considering building a new house nearby. Lennox was already familiar with the architect's work, as his old family home, Kincaid House, had been remodelled by Hamilton in 1812. This symmetrical, neo-Gothic house, with its combination of pointed windows and round-headed openings, is characteristic of his early work, prior to the bolder castellated neo-Gothic of the next decade, seen in buildings such as Castle Toward (1820), and Castle House, Dunoon (1822). The direct relevance of these projects to Lennox Castle will be discussed later. Other prominent works by Hamilton were close to the estate of Woodhead: for instance, Hamilton's second, realised scheme of 1826 for the High Church of Campsie, in the heart of Lennoxtown, or the more distant Airth Castle, to which Hamilton added a new front in 1807–9 (for T. G. Stirling). So it may well have been Lennox's knowledge of Hamilton's accomplishments in that region that secured him the commission.

BUILDING CHRONOLOGY AND PLAN

No original drawings of Lennox Castle are known to exist, but the specifications, contracts and accounts, from early 1837 until late 1842, survive in various forms.[16] From these a thorough chronology of events surrounding the building, decoration, and furnishing of the Castle can be established. Only some of the participants and dates are important to this study, and the roles of architect, decorator and client can be evaluated briefly. From this analysis, it becomes clear that the Castle was a very important and large-scale project, for both Lennox and Hamilton.

Following the building of the stable block and offices, David Hamilton, and his son James (d. 1862), are first documented in April 1837 in relation to the new Castle,[17] and correspondence between Lennox and the Hamiltons continues until June 1842. Hamilton provided the specifications for mason work (which was carried out by James Dick and completed in October 1840), carpenter work (contracted to John Galloway and finished in April 1842), and plaster work (executed by John Leck). All these major contractors were Glasgow-based, whereas the decorators and furniture makers, such as D.R. Hay and Whytock, Reid & Co., were, on the whole, located in Edinburgh. Further research into Hamilton's professional connections within the West may reveal that he employed an established pool of masons, carpenters, and plasterers for much of his work.

One such professional connection is conspicuous at Lennox Castle. William Mossman (1793–1851) was contracted in November 1839, to sculpt an armorial panel to be placed over the north side of the porte cochere. (This is visible in Figure 5.2.) Although only a small commission, this may have been an important one for Mossman, since it was probably his first involvement with Hamilton (and indeed Kincaid Lennox), and may provide a link to the more substantial work he did later. In 1841, Mossman was employed to sculpt the parapet statues for Hamilton's Glasgow and Ship (later Union) Bank on Ingram Street. Lennox himself was one of the proprietors of the Glasgow Ship Bank at that time – although it has been suggested that the cost of building Lennox Castle swallowed up the stock formerly invested in the bank.[18]

The Glasgow–Edinburgh professional divide within the project may also have stemmed from the division of responsibility between Lennox and his wife Frances, who appears to have had control over the furnishing of the Castle. Frances liaised with her sister Lilias Bonar, of Warriston House (East) in Edinburgh, who subsequently dealt with Whytock and others. This was partly due to convenience, but was also, perhaps, a result of Frances' acute deafness.

The scale and importance of the project, the obvious cost of fine materials, inside and out, and the care and attention given to decoration and furnishings, are evident in the specifications and accounts. Another highly unusual indication of Lennox's almost obsessive commitment to this project was provided in the elaborate 'ceremonial of founding and naming of the new castle at Woodhead', held on the 13 March 1838.[19] Building had been in progress since the previous October, and was now, according to the prepared notice for the newspapers, well

5.2 Lennox Castle, north front, c.1900. (Strathkelvin District Library)

advanced: 'the architect presented Mr Lennox a plate to be deposited in the part of the walls where he stood, in a buttress of one of the great towers'.[20] Almost three hundred people assembled on the walls, of which one hundred were masons, carpenters and labourers.

The newspaper notice set out quite an elaborate account of the castle's expected appearance and status, when eventually completed:

> a more appropriate situation for a great family castellated mansion can hardly
> be conceived. The architect, Mr David Hamilton, whose numerous splendid
> designs, including Hamilton Palace and the Glasgow Exchange, have done so
> much to embellish his country, has been happy in lending his style, the
> Norman Gothic of the time to the bold outlines of the surrounding scenery.[21]

The notice claimed that 'the architect has wisely been allowed to adopt in his design the style and extent of subject that he can'[22] – an indication that Hamilton had a reasonable autonomy in the design of the castle. It emphasised the regularity of the composition: 'Each side of the building presents a regular front'.[23] We will return to discuss this feature later. And, finally, it proclaimed the status of the project: 'As a whole, this Castle when finished will not be surpassed it is believed in correctness of architectural composition, in beauty of external ornament, or in excellence of internal arrangement by any private house in Scotland'.[24]

In conjunction with the above building schedule, there was an extensive programme of decoration and fitting out of the castle. D. R. Hay, 'Decorative Painter to the Queen', was contracted to decorate the entire building, inside and out, in September 1840, and his accounts provide an interesting record of the scope of his profession.[25] This included, for example, the painting of 23 mock windows, gilding of clocks, and actually restoring some of Lennox's paintings and furniture. The most fashionable furniture makers were employed, as discussed earlier, and in addition items were brought from Paris and Boulogne, where Frances Lennox lived during the majority of the earlier construction of the castle.

Frances's later letters of 1841, give an insight into not only the various activities but also the professional rivalries of the furniture makers. In one letter she claims:

> Our painting gets on rapidly but I may say my ear is pained my soul is sick with the upholsterers they are so selfish and cry down each others goods ... how horrid it is to hear men of education like Trotter, & Patterson in Glasgow stoop to say such things of Whyttock and his goods.[26]

At one stage she recounts that there are 'nine separate trades working in the house'.[27] And finally on 30 April 1841 she writes that 'here we are in the Castle since last Wednesday – such bustle, such fatigue I never encountered ... we have just the children's three rooms to live in and we are truly glad of them'.[28] The details of the decoration and furniture, are however, outwith the scope of this article.

ARCHITECTURAL ANALYSIS

In this section, we will briefly examine the plan, architectural composition, and detailing of the castle, to set it in the context of Hamilton's own work, the traditions from which it evolved, and the wider development of mid-nineteenth-century revivalism. Fortunately, Lennox Castle has survived relatively unaltered, as very few structural changes were made to the building when it became a mental institution in 1927. During recent dereliction, however, many internal features and fittings – including the main staircase, the ornate ceilings, the hall chimneypiece and the enamelled glass – were damaged or removed.[29]

The castle (Figure 5.3) is approached from the north-east: the drive leads to the arched, vaulted and turreted porte-cochere of the north front. This porch directly enters the main feature of the north front, the five-storey tower (Figure 5.2). The entrance hall is reached by a staircase vestibule, with wide stone steps. From this hall, there is an uninterrupted view along the wide, ninety-foot long grand corridor (Figure 5.4). To the east of this corridor lie the main public rooms: the dining room, library, and (aligned north-south) drawing-room. The family suite is situated in the south-west corner, and Lennox's offices were probably to the west of the entrance hall.

This layout, with the entrance at one end, gives the principal rooms an uninterrupted view, not disturbed by passing visitors, towards the Campsie Hills to the east. In addition, those visiting the house on business could be quickly herded into Lennox's offices without entering the privileged spaces. Finally the family quarters, situated at the back, have the maximum amount of privacy. A similar plan had previously been used by William Burn, in

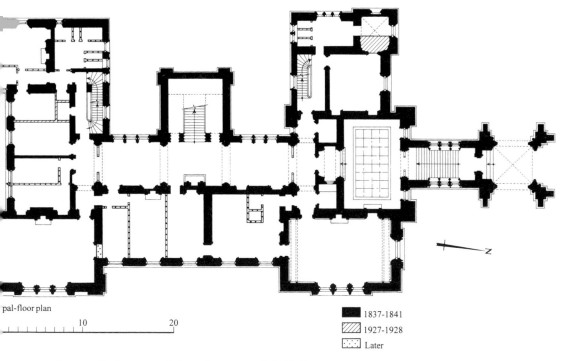

10   20

■ 1837-1841
▨ 1927-1928
⬚ Later

5.3 Lennox Castle, principal floor plan, 1994. (RCAHMS)

5.4 Lennox Castle, principal corridor, 1954. (RCAHMS)

5.5 Lennox Castle, south front, c. 1900. (Strathkelvin District Library)

houses such as Camperdown, of 1821, Ratho, of 1824, and later at Whitehill in 1839. In a desire for privacy, the entrance was not placed symmetrically on the front, but instead set on the flank. Hamilton used this arrangement again on a smaller scale, at Brooksby House, Largs (1840; attributed). As already indicated, the dominant feature of the north front is the entrance tower. This arrangement is common in mid-nineteenth-century houses, but the tower at Lennox Castle clearly evolves from Hamilton's early work. In this there is a marked continuity from his Adam-influenced early houses, such as the entrance tower on the new north-west front at Airth Castle of 1807–9, which is developed later at Castle Toward of 1822. Lennox is the culmination of this development, but its striking verticality may owe more to the choice of the neo-Romanesque as a style; this question will be discussed later.

The east front comprises a central portion of three storeys, set between towers which rise one storey higher. The south front has a similar composition (Figure 5.5). The near-symmetrical arrangement, and the advance and recess of the blocks, looks back, again, to the picturesque composition of Castle Toward. Yet, as we saw above, at Lennox 'each side of the building presents a regular front'.[30] This fact places Lennox within the tradition of

5.6 Lennox Castle, watercolour by Margaret Bonar, c.1850. (Mrs Zela Ashford)

the Adam-castellated style, in houses such as Dalquharran (1790) and Stobs (1792), rather than the picturesque castles common in the early nineteenth century in Scotland. On the west, a low range of offices and outbuildings, of one and two storeys, encloses a small court-yard. The main, five-storey stair-tower projects into the centre of this courtyard, again regularising the composition (see Figure 5.3). This elevational formation, using near-symmetrical end towers set forward on the main front, remained popular until the middle decades of the nineteenth century, and can be seen at, for example, Peddie and Kinnear's Glenmayne, Selkirkshire, of 1866, and Crawfordton, Dumfrieshire, of 1863.[31] A small watercolour painted probably in the 1850s by Frances Lennox's niece, Margaret Bonar,[32] seemingly the earliest surviving view of the castle, shows that it was also originally sur-rounded by seven-foot-high ramparts (Figure 5.6). At some points these projected eighteen feet from the base of the wall. The ramparts were removed in 1927.

The architectural detailing of Lennox Castle has similarities with Hamilton's other work, but, as at Dunlop House (1833), the choice of revivalist style dictates the form. In addition, Lennox himself may have suggested particular heraldic motifs for carved decoration. Most of the windows are round-headed single openings grouped in pairs or threes: for instance, the main eastern windows of the principal floors. These triple lights project slightly, with a dentilated frieze and angle shafts, but above this level, with few exceptions, the windows have moulded jambs and hood moulds. Hamilton had previously used hood moulds at Craw-ford Priory (1809) and Castle House, Dunoon (1822). Similarly the stops of carved human heads, found mainly on the principal and first floor windows of the east front, resemble those at Castle Toward (1820). The groupings of the windows, and other features on the north front, will be discussed later in relation to possible Romanesque models.

The treatment of the corners of the main components, the towers and port cochere, gives Lennox Castle a distinctly vertical emphasis and planar quality. For example, most of the corners feature applied pilaster-like buttresses (on the central stair tower) or shafts (on the north wing of the east front), and often the pilasters themselves contain shafts in their outer angles (on the north tower). In addition, the verticality of the north tower is emphasised by terminating the corner pilasters with square turrets: a common device of Hamilton's.

The castle's rigid consistency of detail is extended to the level of heraldic decoration. The rose (the main heraldic symbol of the ancient Earl of Lennox), and the Kincaid star are given equal importance throughout. These motifs are used, for instance, on Mossman's heraldic panel on the porte-cochere, on the continuous corbelling below the parapet of the east front, on several internal cornices, and as a pattern of the enamelled glass (which now only survives in the principal corridor).

ARCHITECTURAL STYLE

According to Cameron, Lennox's hopes of regaining the title of Earl of Lennox spurred him and his advisers, including Hamilton, to build a new castle in a 'Norman style of archi-tecture', with the explicit aim of evoking the Lennox family's roots.[33] Although Lennox actually claimed that those roots lay in the Saxon rather than the Norman period, the dis-tinction between the two was relatively unimportant in this country (unlike England).

Hamilton may have obliged his patron by suggesting the neo-Norman – more usually referred to today as the 'neo-Romanesque' – as a suitable style. So the choice of style for Lennox Castle may have been greatly influenced by the specific circumstances of the com-mission. However, there was also a wider architectural context. By the early nineteenth century, in several Northern European countries, the search for romantic or non-classical styles was leading away from Gothic, towards a picturesque, round-arched architecture. This would draw on national and Lombardian sources, as well as on the Italian culture of the Quattrocento. In Germany, for instance, its main protagonists were Heinrich Huebsch and Ludwig Persius. Huebsch, in the 1820s, argued for a modern style based on Romanesque (*Rundbogenstil*), and found his sources in the Romanesque abbeys of southern Germany. Persius, on the other hand, drew on Roman, Florentine, and Lombardian sources in designing buildings such as the Friedenskirche in Potsdam (1843–8),

Like these Continental buildings, Lennox Castle cannot claim to be an archaeologically correct revival of any Romanesque original style. It was not intended to be. But some motifs can be fairly precisely attributed. The most likely source was the twelfth-century Kelso

5.7 Kelso Abbey, north transept. (R. W. Billings, *The Baronial and Ecclesiastical Antiquities of Scotland*, 1845–52)

Abbey.[34] Its north transept window groupings are echoed in the triple windows of Lennox's north entrance tower, whose overall arrangement is generally evocative of a Romanesque cathedral front (Figure 5.7). In addition, the arrangement of corner pilaster/buttresses with shafts in the outer angles, found in the north tower of Lennox, is a typical arrangement of the late Romanesque transitional period, and is seen at Kelso. The original sources for any archaeological motifs at Lennox are therefore ecclesiastical rather than domestic, and freely mix early and transitional Romanesque detailing.

In nineteenth-century Scotland, neo-Romanesque was mainly employed in ecclesiastical buildings, such as John Henderson's North Church at Stirling of 1841, and Gillespie Graham's Chapel of St Anthony, at Murthly, of 1845. Although Hamilton only employed this style once, here at Lennox, his initial interest in the Romanesque was taken further by his pupil, Charles Wilson (1810–63). Wilson joined Hamilton in 1827, establishing his own practice in 1837, before Lennox Castle was begun. He followed Hamilton in using details from Kelso's north transept doorway, as a source for his neo-Romanesque gateway to the Southern Necropolis, Glasgow (1840) (Figure 5.8). Like the German architects, Wilson then went on to develop a distinctive round-arched Italian style. This echoed the vertical quality of Lennox Castle in the soaring towers, with elongated triple arches, of his Free Church College in Glasgow (1856–7).

5.8 Charles Wilson, the Southern Necropolis Gateway, 1840. (RCAHMS)

A different problem was posed by the design of country houses, where a picturesque arrangement, medieval connotations and imposing silhouette was required. Here the bold and near-symmetrical design of Lennox seems at first glance inconsistent. To explain this, we need to consider a major innovation that had already taken place in Scottish domestic architecture. Whereas the main stream of picturesque domestic architecture, in Scotland, as much as in other countries, such as England and Germany, had tended towards a horizontal, informal arrangement. Scotland had seen in the Adam castles of the late eighteenth century an attempt to work out a more vertical, symmetrical, compact pattern. In the 1830s Hamilton was making a similar attempt, breaking from the picturesque asymmetry and horizontality of Castle Toward (1820), towards a stronger verticality and an attempt to use Scottish stylistic sources. He tried to do this in two ways. The first was through the Romanesque of Lennox Castle, and the second was the Scots Jacobean of Dunlop House (1831–4).[35] Of these, the neo-Romanesque strand would not directly lead anywhere, other than to isolated examples such as the picturesque addition to Dunimarle by R. & R. Dickson in 1840. But the Scots Renaissance of Dunlop would feed directly into the Baronial, which was to be the dominant domestic-architectural style of the mid- and late nineteenth century.

In conclusion, we can view Lennox Castle's architectural style as an unconventional, but memorable diversion from the mainstream of development in early nineteenth-century Scottish domestic architecture, which led from the Adam castle style to the Baronial.

The Royal Commission on the Ancient and Historical Monuments of Scotland

ACKNOWLEDGEMENTS

I would like to thank Mrs Zela Ashford (for access to family letters), Neil M. Cameron, Ian Gow, Aonghus MacKechnie, Don Martin and Geoffrey Stell. I would also like to thank all my colleagues at RCAHMS who have helped in preparing material for this article.

The author and the AHSS gratefully acknowledge the financial assistance of RCAHMS in the production of this article.

NOTES

1. I. McIvor, *Castellated and Gothic Houses in Scotland, 1745–1840: Report to the Historic Buildings Council*, 1964.

2. See also A. Rowan, 'Notes on the The Georgian Gothic Style in Scotland', *Castellated and Gothic Houses in Scotland, 1745–1840*. This particular view was typical of its time, and it would be fair to say that the authors will have doubtless revised their opinions on the subject. By contrast, Hamilton's work at Dunlop in 1833 is cited by Walker as a return to a Scots Jacobean

dormant since George Sanders' alterations to Scone Palace in the 1790s. See
also D. M. Walker, 'Scone Palace', in Howard Colvin and John Harris (ed.),
The Country Seat, Studies in the History of the British Country House, 1970; and the
substantial account of Lennox Castle in the Royal Commission on the Ancient
and Historical Monuments of Scotland (RCAHMS), *Stirlingshire, An Inventory of
the Ancient Monuments*, vol. 2, 1963, no. 324.

3. J. Cameron, *The Parish of Campsie, Sketches and Incidents*, Kirkintilloch,
1892, p. 163.

4. Letter from Willamina Cunninghame to Mrs Lilias Bonar, 5 March 1832,
indicates that Kincaid Lennox was in the process of moving to Woodhead
House, before he had officially succeeded to the estate. Letters in the
possession of Mrs Zela Ashford, originating from John Lennox Kincaid
Lennox's wife Francis, third daughter of John Cunninghame of Craigends, and
members of her immediate family.

5. A brief history, description and plan of this ruin is provided in RCAHMS,
Stirlingshire, no. 205.

6. 'Proposed Alterations, Stables and Farm Offices at Woodhead House',
Records of the Lennox Family of Woodhead, Strathclyde Regional Council Archives
(SCRA), T-LX/15/56.

7. J. Cameron, *The Parish of Campsie*, p. 162.

8. Letter from William Bonar of Woodhead to Andrew Bonar Esq.,
Edinburgh, 15 September 1832. From letters in possession of Mrs Zela
Ashford.

9. R. Hamilton, *Case of Margaret Lennox of Woodhead in relation to the Title,
Honours and Dignity of the Ancient Earls of Levenax or Lennox*, Edinburgh, 1813.

10. Ibid.

11. J. Cameron, *The Parish of Campsie*, p. 164.

12. Ibid., p. 162.

13. *Records of the Lennox Family*, SCRA, T-LX/12/2.

14. Ibid.

15. Dundas and Wilson CS, *Particulars, Plans and Conditions of Sale of The Lennox
Castle Estate*, Edinburgh, 1927; A. L. Ritchie, *Lennox Castle Mental Defectives'
Institution*, Glasgow, 1936.

16. *Records of the Lennox Family*, SCRA, T-LX/12/2; also detailed in a bound
volume, *Lennox Castle Buildings, Estimates and Specifications*, 1837, Strathkelvin
District Library, Kirkintilloch.

17. James Hamilton appears to have been in partnership with his father during
the latter's last years. H. Colvin, *A Biographical Dictionary of British Architects
1600–1840*, 1978, p. 380.

18. J. Cameron, *The Parish of Campsie*, p. 164.

19. John Lennox Kincaid Lennox, 'Considerations regarding the propriety of
a little ceremonial by way of founding and naming the new castle at
Woodhead', 26 March 1838, *Records of the Lennox Family*, SCRA, T-LX/12/8.

20. 'Notice for Newspaper Regarding Lennox Castle', 3 April 1839, *Records of
the Lennox Family*, SCRA, T-LX/12/8.

21. Ibid.

22. Ibid.

23. Ibid.

24. Ibid.

25. 'Account of Painter Work at Lennox Castle by Mr D.R. Hay, September 1841', and 'Additional Account of Painter at Lennox Castle by Mr D.R. Hay, 1840', *Lennox Castle Buildings, Estimates and Specifications*, Strathkelvin District Library. For D. R. Hay, see I. Gow, *The Scottish Interior*, Edinburgh, 1992.

26. Letter from Frances Kincaid Lennox to Lilias Bonar, 23 March 1841. From letters in possession of Mrs Zela Ashford.

27. Letter from Frances Kincaid Lennox to Lilias Bonar, 4 April 1841, as above.

28. Letter from Frances Kincaid Lennox to Lilias Bonar, 30 April 1841, as above.

29. 'Memorandum respecting the Tablet in Lennox Castle', 27 February 1838, contained in *Records of the Lennox Family* written by Lennox, provides an insight into his relationship with Hamilton. Lennox writes that 'Mr Hamilton still expresses a strong desire that a stone tablet be placed in the hall over the chimney piece. He says it is of great consequence on point of producing an appropriateness in the architectural effect intended. In this case it would be best to let him be the judge ... but there is one particular that I think should not be conceded to him in the matter. He wants to inscribe upon it "waste not want not" ...'. Lennox objects to this, and suggests a quote from the Bible, but Hamilton's joke translates as a criticism of Lennox's excesses in building the Castle.

30. 'Notice for Newspaper Regarding Lennox Castle', *Records of the Lennox Family*.

31. Original drawings for Crawfordton are in the collection of the NMRS.

32. Original watercolour in the possession of Mrs Zela Ashford.

33. J. Cameron, *The Parish of Campsie*, p. 163.

34. I am indebted here to my colleague, Neil M. Cameron, who has suggested possible Romanesque sources for Lennox Castle, and for the later work of Hamilton's pupil Charles Wilson (1810–63).

35. D. M. Walker has suggested that the key Scots Renaissance characteristics of Dunlop House derive from Hamilton's personal study of Old College, Glasgow: see Walker, 'Notes on Architects', National Monuments Record of Scotland.

TATIANA RUCHINSKAYA

William Hastie and the Reconstruction of Moscow after the 1812 Fire

A new era in the history of town planning in Moscow came into being at the beginning of the nineteenth century. In 1812 a huge fire destroyed whole areas of the city, and as a consequence, an era of reconstruction began.

A SKILFUL ARCHITECT was needed for the new planning of Moscow. Czar Alexander I appointed William Hastie, a Scotsman who was already the chief architect of Tsarskoe Selo, the 'Tsar's village' near St Petersburg.[1] His original project, dated 15 July 1813, has been lost. But these proposals were recorded by the 'Committee for Buildings' in 1814[2] and have been preserved in the Moscow Military Archive.

In shaping the city, Hastie thought primarily in terms of squares. He envisaged a semi-circular chain of them running along the ring roads around the Kremlin, Kitai Gorod and Beli Gorod (Figure 6.1). The squares were to be placed at the junction of the radial streets and ring roads, and further out at the Zemlianoi Gorod ring road, at the intersection of the radial streets and old rampart. In most instances he proposed the adaptation of existing, irregular public spaces into formal public spaces of great geometrical diversity.

As a Scottish architect, Hastie would have been familiar with the features of the British eighteenth-century city – with the crescent and circus, as well as the grid and the square. It was this language, used in cities from Bath to Glasgow and from Edinburgh to Exeter, that Hastie tried to introduce to Moscow. However, it was an unfamiliar language in that city. Moscow was built on an irregular street pattern which often opened up into large, deep and unstructured spaces. Part of Hastie's task was to adapt this informal structure to the norms of Georgian urban ensembles. Thus he designed large squares with axial routes running through or from them (Figures 6.2b and 6.3d), just as he had seen in Craig's proposals for Edinburgh or in Glasgow's new grid. He also tried to group town houses in such a way as to give the effect of single palaces in the main squares, for example in Red Square (Figure 6.2a). On the other hand, Hastie also showed some respect for Moscow's own traditions. Many of his town houses had two sections: the first, right on the edge of the street, and the second, set back. His designs also allowed for spaces between the houses and gave an informal character to many of the streets which was more in keeping with Moscow's picturesque tradition. On the other hand, the general tendency of his proposals, towards the regularisation of the city, did cause considerable difficulties.

On 17 October 1813, Hastie put his project before the Moscow Committee for Buildings. There were several objections to his design. The semi-circular and polygonal spaces that he proposed were on privately owned land and paid little attention to the existing fabric

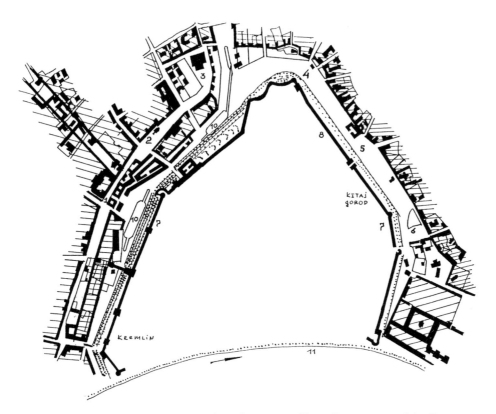

6.1 Projects for squares around the Kremlin and Kitai Gorod by William Hastie and the Committee for Buildings. (The black line indicates Hastie's project, the dotted line, that of the Committee for Buildings.) *Key*: 1. Mohovaya Square; 2. Ohotnij Riad Square; 3. Theatre Square; 4. Nikoliskaya Square; 5. Iljinskaya Square; 6. Varvarskaya Square; 7. The wall of the Kremlin; 8. The wall of Kitai Gorod; 9. Boulevards; 10. River Neglinaya; 11. Moscow River. (Author)

of the city. Land was very expensive and purchase by the state was out of the question. His squares were broad and the new streets destroyed and fragmented the existing housing estates.

The difficulties arose not only because of the irregularities of the city plan but also because those irregularities were in part dictated by a number of topographical peculiarities of Moscow that have influenced the form of the city to this day. Moscow is built on seven hills and a number of rivers. Fields, meadows and pastures linked with the open spaces of the suburbs and blurred the edges of the city. So close was this relationship between city and countryside that at the end of the eighteenth century the architect Nicolai Ljvov could aptly characterise Moscow as a 'Garden City'. It reflected the order of nature. The buildings climbed the slopes and took the bends as best they could. Moscow buildings stood in an organic relationship to the ground; they looked like growing plants.

Visual parallels between some organisms and town plans were hard to resist. The paralleling of human organs with urban elements affirmed the importance of urban life. Open spaces like squares and parks were the lungs of Moscow, and the centre was the heart, pumping blood though the arteries (the streets). However, in classical terms the town space was understood as a rational geometrical environment for the buildings and in seeking to establish this, Hastie showed a concern with classical values, which were integral to European society from late antiquity onwards through the nineteenth century.

There survive two main plans for the reconstruction of Moscow after the fire of 1812. Great attention in both was given to the squares near the Kremlin. The principle of orientating new classical squares and monuments to the historical centre was born. In spite of the stylistic difference, the system of regular Moscow squares was subordinated to the ancient Kremlin[3] and the regularity of the one was contrasted with the dynamics of the older monuments. Thus, a classical element was introduced into the more Russian traditions of irregular town space.

Red Square was widened (Figure 6.2). The edge of the market was to be pushed back behind the Places of the Presence,[4] and the moat was to be destroyed. The Committee for Buildings had a different idea: boulevards would run alongside the Kremlin wall and the old edge of the market would be preserved (as planned by O. Bove).[5] Thus the excessive width of this square would be diminished, with the Places of the Presence – with its tower – kept as an architectural accent on the north side.

Hastie intended the square near the temple of Vasili Blajeni as a continuation of Red Square. The ancient temple would be open on each side. The Committee for Buildings, on the other hand, wanted to open the temple only from the higher side – that is to say, from the Red Square side – thus creating a contrast between the temple and its surrounds in keeping with the Russian traditional system.

The Committee for Buildings planned a new Theatre Square (Figure 6.1/3) in relation to the ancient wall of Kitai Gorod. This involved the destruction of the surrounding buildings in order to open more space, and the culverting of the River Neglinaya. Theatre Square created a connecting zone in which newly erected classical buildings and ancient monuments co-existed.

The curved edge of Nicolskaya Square (Figure 6.1/4) was pushed back, and Varvarskaya Square (Figure 6.1/6) was symmetrically positioned at the other end of the boulevard.

Hastie wanted to destroy Mohovaya Square (Figure 6.1/1). The Committee for Buildings, however, only widened it to 10 sazhens.[6] As the bastions and moat were destroyed, this square was expanded towards the Kremlin wall and connected with Moiseevskaya and Ohotnij Riad (Figure 6.1/2) Squares. These squares created a classical façade opposite the Kremlin and Kitai Gorod.

Hastie had designed fourteen octagonal squares at the entries to the city, but because of their distance from the centre the Committee for Buildings paid no attention to them.

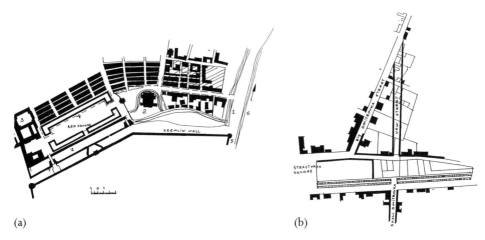

(a)   (b)

6.2 (a) Plan of Red Square according to Hastie's project and the Committee for Buildings proposal.
  Key: 1. The moat; 2. Temple of Vasili Blajeni; 3. The building of the Places of Presence; 4. The
  edge of the market; 5. Boulevards; 6. River Moscow (Author). (b) Hastie's design for the new
  street near Strastraya Square. (Author)

The squares on the junction of the main roads were regulated. Hastie proposed a square
be built near the Slobodskoj Palace (Figure 6.3(a)) on church land and private estates. The
church had to be demolished and the existing dwellings pushed out.

From the point of view of the Committee for Buildings, the main requirement was that
of functionality. They needed squares for markets and for religious and civic gatherings. Out
of Hastie's proposals to build ten market squares (Figure 6.3) the Committee for Building
chose seven, and from thirteen church squares (Figure 6.4), they chose seven.

Arbatskaya Square was a market square (Figure 6.3(b)). The Committee planned to en-
large it to the beginning of Prechistenskij Boulevard. Hastie had proposed another market
square nearby, but this was rejected.

At the square of the Red Gates, Hastie proposed a huge rectangular space but this was
rejected by the Committee in favour of a development of the existing large triangular square
(Figure 6.3(d)). On the other hand, his grandiose proposals for the enlargement of
Serpuhovskaya Square (Figure 6.3(c)) was accepted on the sensible grounds that the three
existing markets that were situated within the proposed expansion zone could be accommodated in the new square.

In the new church squares (Figure 6.4) the same tension between Russian and Western
European tradition is evident. Hastie, possibly influenced by Glasgow church squares,
wanted to place the churches in the centre of his squares. Perhaps it was hard for him to
understand that Russian churches were usually located on the corners of main streets or in
the middle of blocks, with only the façade visible from the street. The Committee decided
that Hastie's idea of presenting them in the round would be unpopular in the town.

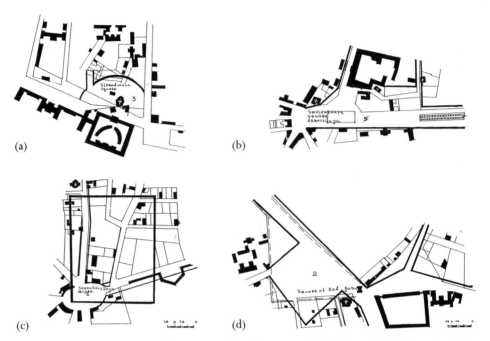

6.3 The market square projects by Hastie and the Committee for Buildings. (Hastie's project is indicated by the black line, that of the Committee for Buildings by the dotted line.) *Key:* (a) Slobodskaya Square; (b) Arbatskaya Square; (c) Serpuhovskaya Square; (d) Red Gate Square. (Author)

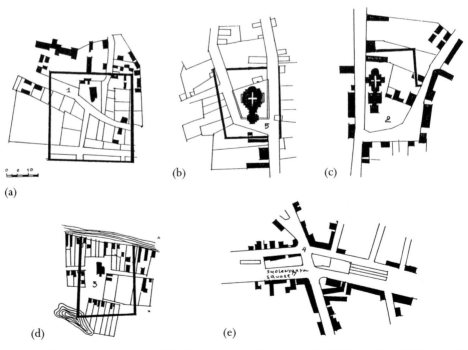

6.4 The church squares, projected by Hastie and the Committee for Buildings. *Key:* (a) the church of Ermolaya; (b) the church of Martin; (c) the church of Nikitji on Old Basmanaya Street; (d) the church on the Pometnij Vrajek Street; (e) the monastery of Zachatia. (Author)

They were similarly unenthusiastic about the three new straight streets in Hastie's plan, that connected the centre with the entry squares. The first of these was from Small Nikitskaya Street to Big Presnenskaya Street; the second from Big to Small Dmitrovka (Figure 6.2); and the third from the beginning of Big Nikitskaya to the Tverskie Gates, through the existing buildings.

In this, and throughout the whole project, compromise was necessary so that, in the end, a new Moscow emerged that was not simply based on Western ideas but on a synthesis of traditional and Classical principles. It is obvious that, in consultation with the Committee for Buildings, William Hastie created a new architectural approach to the typical Russian town.

NOTES

1. A. Schmidt, 'William Hastie – Scottish planner of Russian towns', *Proceedings of the American Philosophical Society*, vol. 114, 1970, pp. 226–43; M. Korshunova, 'W. Hastie in Russia', *Architectural History*, vol. 17, 1974; Dmitri Shuidkovsky 'Classical Edinburgh and Russian Town Planning of the late 18th and early 19th centuries: the role of William Hastie', *Architectural Heritage*, vol. 2, 1991, pp. 69–78.

2. This Committee for Buildings was established by the state to produce regular plans for the improvement of Moscow.

3. N. Gulianitski, 'The architectural methods of Russian classicism', *Architectural Heritance*, no. 22, Moscow, 1974; A. Feodorov-Davjidov, *The Architecture of Moscow after the 1812 Fire*, Moscow, 1953.

4. The name of the building for administration in Moscow, like a townhall.

5. Bove worked in the Committee for Buildings. See Z. Pokrovskaya, *O. Bove*, Moscow, 1964.

6. 1 sazhen = 2 metres (approx.).

7.1 Gribloch House, entrance elevation. (*Country Life*)

CAROLINE A. MACGREGOR

Gribloch: The Evolution of the Architectural and Interior Design of a 1930s Scottish Country House

Although Sir Basil Spence is recognised as one of our greatest twentieth-century architects, little has been written about his early work, particularly his pre-war Scottish country houses. This study of one such house, Gribloch, is based on original drawings and on correspondence between Spence, his clients John and Helen Colville, and their numerous 'consultants', notably Nikolaus Pevsner, the American architect Perry M. Duncan, and the interior designer John Hill. The resultant house, which preserves much of its original interior decor and landscaped setting, is a unique fusion of Regency and Modernist styles.

GRIBLOCH HOUSE (Figure 7.1) stands in a commanding position one mile north-west of the village of Kippen in Stirlingshire. The house was the centre of a newly created 1,379-acre estate, situated 568 feet above sea-level, enjoying panoramic views over the upper Forth Valley to the Grampian Mountains. To quote Spence himself, Gribloch is a large country house 'of the 16 bedroom variety'.[1] It is a two-storied, white-harled struc-ture below a low-pitched copper roof, with a distinctive inverted 'F'-shaped plan. The front of the house faces north, giving each of the rooms on this elevation spectacular views over the Grampians, from Ben Cleuch in the east to Ben Lomond in the west. Two south-facing splayed wings enclose a swimming pool. A tree-lined avenue affords views of the Fintry Hills to the south.

Gribloch was built in 1938–9. It was one of four Scottish country houses designed by Basil Spence (1907–76) whilst he was a partner in Rowand Anderson Paul and Partners in Edinburgh. Spence had joined the firm in 1935, fourteen years after Sir Rowand Anderson's death. His clients for Gribloch were John M. Colville (1903–84) and his American wife, Helen (1908–77).

John Colville was the grandson of David Colville who founded the well-known Scottish steel-producing company of the same name. He was appointed works manager of Dalzell Steel Works in Motherwell in 1932.[2] He met his wife, Helen Markillie of San Francisco, California, in January 1934 whilst on a business tour of America and returned in December of the same year to marry her.[3] Allied to his industrial interests John Colville was involved in design matters and served on the Scottish Standing Committee of the Council for Art and Industry for several years, becoming Vice Chairman and convenor of the industrial com-mittee. The Scottish Committee, which was set up in April 1934, was a sub-section of the Council for Art and Industry. Its aim was to bring Art and Industry closer together in order to improve the design of goods and to make them more saleable here and abroad. Both

Committees included some of the best designers and architects of the day, including Basil Spence, Oliver Hill and E. McKnight Kauffer.[4] Colville also represented the Scottish Committee on the Board of Governors of Glasgow School of Art and was actively involved in the Empire Exhibition in Glasgow.[5]

Although there is no written record of why the Colvilles chose Spence to design their new house it is reasonable to assume that John Colville and Spence met through their work for the Empire Exhibition, particularly in the year leading up to its opening on 3 May 1938. The Scottish Standing Committee, of which both men were members, was given the task of constructing, equipping and furnishing a model country house. Furthermore, in April 1937 Colville was appointed to the Scottish National Committee which was to erect and furnish two Scottish Pavilions.[6] Spence designed both buildings in collaboration with the Exhibition architect, Thomas Tait. John Colville may also have seen Spence's scheme for the Imperial Chemical Industries (ICI) Pavilion, which was the result of a competition.

Without doubt Spence also came to the Colvilles' attention through a shooting lodge at Quothquhan, near Biggar in Lanarkshire, which he had recently designed for John Colville's cousin, Christian Hendrie and her husband, Alexander Erskine-Hill, MP. The two commissions overlapped one another. As correspondence between Erskine-Hill and Spence regarding the construction of Quothquhan tailed off in August 1937, so the surviving letters between Colville and Spence began: Spence's first scheme for Gribloch dates from 5 August 1937.

The Colvilles were later to call upon the services of a New York architect, Perry M. Duncan, who was retained as 'consultant architect' in December 1937.[7] A letter from Mrs Colville to Spence, written some months later reveals why she (and her husband) had taken this unusual and costly step: 'As you must know, I feel that the additional expense of employing another architect would have been absolutely unnecessary under different circumstances, but it seemed the only thing to do as the plans at that time had come to a dead end.'[8] The Colvilles felt that the plans for their house had been, and were continuing to be neglected: 'It is not that we have ever doubted your ability, it is simply that you do not seem to have the necessary time to devote to our plans'. The Colvilles desire to get Gribloch finished as quickly as possible may have stemmed from concern that war might break out before the house was finished and delay its completion. As it was, the house was not occupied until 16 December 1939, several months after war had been declared.[9] Moreover, the Colvilles were without a home of their own at this time. Their previous house, Auchengray, near Caldercruix in Lanarkshire had been destroyed by fire in March 1937.[10] Since then they had been resident in Kippen, staying at John Colville's family home, Arngomery.

The Colvilles thought that Spence was too busy with the Empire Exhibition. Mrs Colville's letter further reveals that she and her husband had asked Spence 'months ago' to let another architect design Gribloch's entrance-lodge and garage-block so that Spence would have more time to devote to the house. However, Duncan was asked to prepare 'revised drawings' of the house itself, based on Spence's plans and elevations. Duncan duly submitted his drawings to the Colvilles in January 1938. Spence, meanwhile, was asked to design the garage-block, but not the lodge. Owing to what the Colvilles judged to be 'the excessive cost' of Spence's original scheme for the lodge, they made other arrangements.[11] John Colville was so impressed by a modern bungalow near Bannockburn, designed by the Falkirk practice of M. Copland and Blakey, that he commissioned this firm to produce a virtually identical design for Gribloch's entrance-lodge.[12]

Far from speeding up work on the house, Duncan's appointment seems to have caused further delays. Spence clearly felt that by employing another architect to work on the house, rather than on ancillary buildings, the Colvilles were casting doubts on his ability to do the job. The Colvilles meanwhile continued to complain that work on their house was 'unreasonably slow' and that the Exhibition was still taking up too much of Spence's time:

> After all we hope this house will be in existence long after the Exhibition has been pulled down and forgotten, and if it is to be a credit to you, I think greater attention to detail is necessary. I do hope that there can be some kind of equitable understanding because there is more than a year of work yet to be got through and unless it is done in an efficient and businesslike manner there will be so much unnecessary contention for all concerned.[13]

It is not known why the Colvilles selected Duncan. Mrs Colville's letter to Spence merely states that: 'the main thing that recommends Mr. Duncan to John and I is his apparent keen interest and enthusiasm to get on with the work'. According to Lady Hutchison, (the Colvilles' daughter), her parents did not know Duncan well at the time. It is significant that among Mrs Colville's papers there are two undated extracts from American magazines which mention Duncan, and an article featuring his work. The extracts reveal that Duncan received 'an Honorable Mention' from the judges of the *House Beautiful* Eighth Annual Small House Competition and First Prize in the Ninth Competition. The article, which illustrates Duncan's proposed scheme for a small house, states that: 'the plans represent a carefully and deftly executed example of modern design. It is not experimentally modern, though its form is fresh and arresting. On the other hand, it owes little to "period", except in a few of its tongue-in-cheek details.'[14]

There are a number of similarities between this scheme and Gribloch. These include a low-pitched roof behind a parapet-wall, a Colonial-style porch, full-length ground-floor windows and a curved hall overlooking a swimming-pool. Even a Greek-key motif above the entrance of Duncan's small house reappears as a frieze on his 'revised North Elevation' of Gribloch. The Colvilles must have decided that this external treatment was too overtly historical and they reverted to Spence's scheme instead. Spence then wrote back to Duncan, in February 1938, saying that 'the feeling we are striving for is something more of the Regency type, freshened up to fit with modern conditions'.[15] Duncan's involvement with Gribloch was thereafter largely limited to helping with internal planning and sending information and suggested layouts for the kitchen and laundry to the Colvilles.

In addition to employing Spence and Duncan, the Colvilles consulted some of the most talented and innovative British, French, and German designers of the period to work on Gribloch's interiors, including Nikolaus Pevsner, then chief buyer for Gordon Russell Ltd; the prominent London interior designer, John Hill; the furniture designer Betty Joel, and the Parisian Ferronier D'Art, Raymond Subes. The garden meanwhile was laid out by the Surrey-based garden architect, J. E. Grant White.

There is no record of the discussions the Colvilles must have had with Spence regarding the form and appearance of their new house. Apart from the reference in Spence's letter to Duncan, there is no further mention of style in a considerable correspondence. Most of the letters between Colville and Spence concern alterations to existing plans and the practicalities of construction. It is significant, however, that amongst the papers relating to the house are photographs of various country houses from the property pages of *Country Life*. The cuttings date from May and July 1937, the period during which Spence and Colville would have been discussing the various forms the house might take. Spence's first scheme for Gribloch dates from 5 August 1937. Lady Hutchison describes these photographs as showing houses which Spence and her father liked.[16] Amongst this collection of houses (which variously includes a former Benedictine nunnery, an Elizabethan manor and Queen Anne and Georgian country houses) is an advertisement for 'Joldwynds' (Figure 7.2), designed by Oliver Hill in 1933 for the Rt. Hon. Sir Wilfrid Greene, and built on Holmbury Hill near Dorking, Surrey. In the advertisement, Joldwynds is described as a 'stunning conception of the country home of the future'.[17] Joldwynds and Gribloch have obvious similarities, and the former may have inspired Gribloch's circular two-storeyed staircase-window, balconies and swimming-pool. Another less obvious similarity between the two houses lies in their planning. As Christopher Hussey wrote in 1934, Joldwynds

> literally lays itself out to take advantage of every opportunity of position, sun and view. To borrow current jargon it is 'extrovert,' in contrast to the older 'introvert' self-conscious type of house in which the designer's chief consideration was; 'What impression will this house give from outside?' – not 'How can I put the inhabitants most joyously *en rapport* with their surroundings?'[18]

Similar considerations apparently underpinned the design of Gribloch. In a letter to Colville dated 26 August 1937, Spence wrote of 'the fundamental condition you laid down fairly clearly when I last visited you' about combining 'both the view and the sun in the drawing room, living room and dining room, and if possible the staircase and the main bedrooms of all three suites'.[19] Combining the sun and view in the public rooms at Gribloch caused Spence many problems. He experimented with a whole range of outline plans before settling for the inverted 'F'-shaped plan. It is interesting to note that the words 'sun' and 'view' appear within the points of a compass on several of Spences's sketch-plans for Gribloch.

Whilst Joldwynds was perhaps the predominant influence underlying Spence's design for

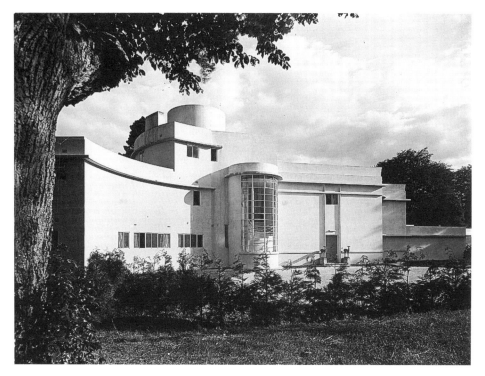

7.2 Oliver Hill, Joldwynds, Holmbury Hill, near Dorking, 1934. (RCAHME)

Gribloch, it was not the only one. Classicism, and in particular the Regency style, was an important source of inspiration too. Regency-derived elements are visible on the exterior. One such example is Spence's use of a rounded bow between the two splayed wings of the house (Figure 7.3). John Nash used a similar device to disguise the joints of streets meeting obliquely and Anthony Blee has been able to confirm that Spence (his father-in-law) was a great admirer of the way Nash turned corners. A further example is the bow-ended form of the living-room, with its balcony and simple railings at first-floor level, which cleverly directs one's eye round the corner of the house. Nash used a similar device at Cronkhill in Shropshire. The roof-treatment is similarly classical in inspiration. It is low-pitched and is partially (and from some angles totally) obscured behind a parapet-wall. This roof-treatment is frequently seen on eighteenth-century houses. Classicism is also evident inside. The drawing-room and dining-room were both furnished with Georgian furniture and have Adam-style fireplaces. The day and night nurseries, servants' hall and one of the guest bed-rooms have Regency style cast-iron hob grates.

In the late summer or early autumn of 1937, Spence submitted a number of watercolour sketch-plans to the Colvilles. One scheme arranged the house around two sides of an entrance forecourt, in an orientation completely different from the executed design. In the

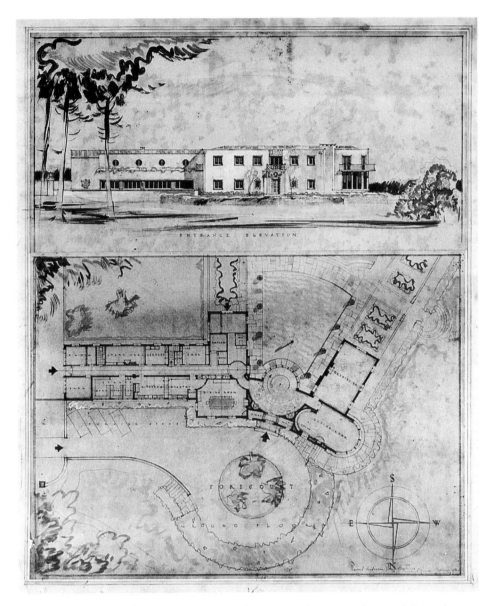

7.3 Basil Spence, Gribloch House, unexecuted entrance elevation and ground-floor plan, 30 September 1937. (RCAHMS)

sketch-plan, the hall and swimming-pool face west; as built, they face south. The convex servants' wing, which is such a distinctive feature of this scheme, was not built though Spence was to use a similar design for the garage block. Despite these differences, this early scheme does include many important features which were later re-arranged and incorporated in the

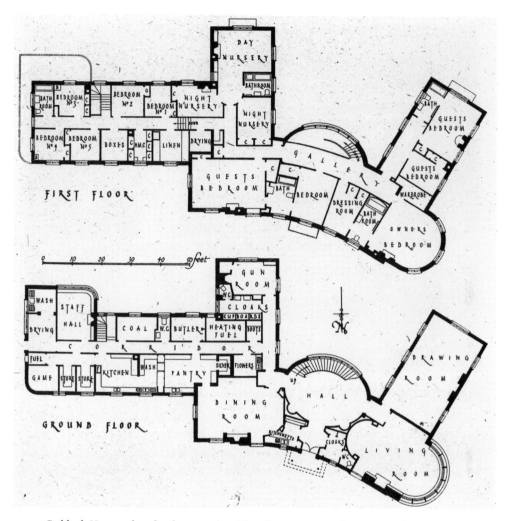

7.4 Gribloch House, plans for the ground and first floor as executed. (*Country Life*)

final design, e.g. the swimming-pool, white-painted walls, curved staircase-window, bow-ended living-room window, balconies, and the low-pitched roof.

The basic shape and appearance of Gribloch were established by 30 September 1937. Nevertheless, a comparison between the drawings of that date (Figure 7.3) and the house as built reveals substantial differences (Figure 7.4). Correspondence confirms that these changes arose from discussions between the Colvilles, Spence and Duncan.

Nowhere is the interplay between the parties better documented or demonstrated than in the changing design of the hall. It is known that Mrs Colville wanted a curved hall. The 'source books' she compiled from articles and extracts from such American magazines as

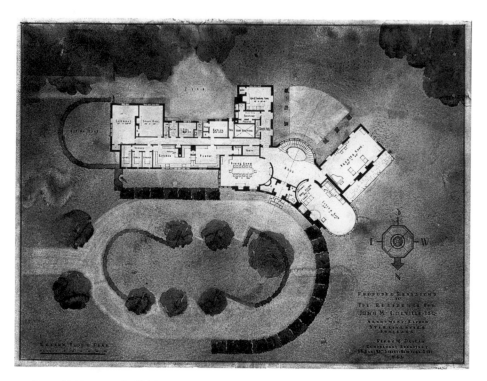

7.5 Perry M. Duncan, Gribloch House, ground-floor plan, January 1938. (RCAHMS)

House and Garden, *House Beautiful* and *Arts and Decoration*, contain three illustrations of curved halls, on one of which she wrote 'Entrance Hall' on the top right corner. Spence's original design for the hall incorporated curved walls, and featured a staircase that may have been inspired by Oliver Hill's staircase design at Joldwynds.

Duncan's ground-floor plan indicates that he proposed radical alterations to the shape and size of the hall (Figure 7.5). In the letter of 12 January 1938 which accompanied his plans, Duncan wrote:

> The main hall which serves these three main rooms is now a shape which definitely expresses the accessibility of the rooms without making the entrances any less private than they were in the original plan. The shape is interesting, unusual, and quite logical. The curve of the stairway has been flattened slightly to conform to the revised hall. This helps the exterior treatment by decreasing the angles formed in the corners by the intersection of the bay.[20]

Duncan also proposed to alter the hall further by increasing the angle between the two south-wings, thereby creating a more open effect and eliminating the wedge shape of the space between the wings. Duncan argued that this change in angle would accentuate the curve in the façade, making it more 'interesting'.

Spence's final design suggests that while he took cognizance of Duncan's implied criticism of his original design, he evolved his own solution. Spence replaced the tight staircase cylinder with an oval, whereas Duncan's revised drawings still incorporated a circular, but wider, staircase. Spence's solution not only softened the appearance of the south elevation, and allowed more light into the interior, but also permitted the creation of a perfectly elliptical entrance-hall. The curve of the north façade remained unchanged. Whilst Spence did design the form of the hall, he was excluded by the Colvilles from having any say in its interior decoration. The interior was designed by John Hill of Green & Abbott Ltd.

Similar interplay between the parties (in this case involving the Colvilles and Spence) is evident in the evolution of the interior planning of the servants' wing and north elevation. The Colvilles gave Spence precise details of their requirements for this wing, particularly the kitchen-quarters. For example, they specified that they wanted the pantry to be 'of generous proportions, leading direct to the dining room, but served by a hatch from the kitchen', and also 'very near the butler's room and the silver and boots should be adjacent'. The servants' hall 'had to be very near the kitchen', and the kitchen was to have a larder and small store next to it.[21] Such ideas may have been gleaned from a leaflet entitled 'Planning Your Home' published by *House Beautiful*.[22] Despite this detailed brief, Spence's original scheme did not meet with the Colvilles' approval. In a note to Spence, John Colville wrote that whilst he and his wife thought the interior of the house was 'most attractive', it was 'not quite as convenient as we would have liked'. He continued 'We are keen to reduce passages to the minimum, especially in the servants wing, and wonder if this could be achieved successfully by putting the passage down the middle, and having this wing slightly wider'. Colville then admitted that 'I have had the audacity to make a sketch plan based as much as possible on yours, and enclose it for your examination'.[23]

Arguably, the alteration which most affected the final appearance of the house was the removal of the sun-deck on the north elevation (Figure 7.3), and the subsequent addition of a curved laundry and staff-hall block, (with balcony above) on the south-east corner. This change must have been the result of further discussions between Spence and the Colvilles for there is no record of Duncan's involvement. Furthermore, it is shown on a model of the house signed and dated 'Rowand Anderson Paul and Partners 20/XI/37', pre-dating Duncan's appointment as 'consultant architect' by about a month.

The entrance elevation was similarly modified by the Colvilles. Spence's early north elevation of 30 September 1937 shows that he intended having square windows on both the ground and first floor of the main block. The servants' wing, meanwhile, was to have a long kitchen-window with four portholes at first-floor level. Spence also intended embellishing the façade with relief sculpture above the front door and also at the end of the servants' wing (Figure 7.3). In a rough note, probably the draft of a letter to Spence, John Colville wrote that he preferred plain walls without ornamentation, high ground-floor windows, portholes, and a steeper roof-line.[24] Spence duly submitted his revised north elevation to Colville on

4 October 1937, but he clearly preferred his original elevation. In the accompanying letter he wrote,

> You will notice the windows on the ground floor have been enlarged, the roof
> steepened and the servants wing altered to your suggestions. I have not shown
> any sculpture on this drawing. I am also sending a print of the original elevation
> so that an accurate comparison may be made between these two solutions. In
> my opinion, the new elevation is inclined to be restless. I like the steep roof,
> but not the porthole at the end of the servants' wing. I still feel that the
> interest should be on the level of the long kitchen window. I also feel that a
> little sculpture is necessary over the front door.[25]

The final elevation indicates that whilst Spence was successful in dissuading John Colville from having a porthole at the end of the servants' wing, his long kitchen window and sculpture were rejected. Spence's feeling that 'a little sculpture' was desirable may be explained by his training as a sculptor before turning to architecture. Throughout his career Spence incorporated sculpture, designed by himself and others, in such buildings as the North Scottish and ICI Pavilions at the Empire Exhibition, Broughton Place, and Coventry Cathedral.

It is clear from the multitude of alternative designs in the NMRS Gribloch collection, that Spence and Colville continued to experiment with different combinations of windows on the north elevation. Spence wanted to make the kitchen windows square, arguing that they gave 'a very restful effect and elevationally are satisfactory'.[26] John Colville opted instead for the present tall oblong windows. Overall, the existing window-arrangement (Figure 7.1) is much more practical than Spence's original scheme. The high ground-floor windows ensure that the interiors are well-lit, which is important since this elevation faces north. Whilst Spence's long kitchen-window would have given a pleasing horizontal emphasis to the house, it would have made the kitchen-quarters cold. There is no denying, however, that the mixture of differently sized and shaped windows does contribute to the feeling of 'restlessness' of which Spence complained. It also tends to fragment the entrance-façade into three distinct parts.

Whilst Spence did his best to accommodate his clients' demands regarding the staff wing and north elevation, he did nevertheless object several times to what he considered to be unreasonable interference by John Colville. Perhaps the best documented example of this is to be found in the case of the wrought-iron grilles on either side of the front door. Spence's studded lattice-work design is visible on his entrance-elevation of 30 September 1937 (Figure 7.3). John Colville decided not to proceed with it, perhaps because of Duncan's criticism of Spence's exterior detailing, which he thought was 'a little light, and tends to be fussy'. Duncan continued 'I realise the ornamental iron grille-work is merely a sketchy indication and will probably change in detailing, however, it looks slightly Spanish which is a curse on a modern house'.[27] As if this criticism from another architect was not bad enough, Colville proceeded to submit his own design to Spence for comment. Not surprisingly,

7.6 John Colville, design for wrought-iron railings on either side of the front door. (Private Collection)

Spence felt that his client was impinging on his territory. On 6 July 1939 he wrote, 'I realise that your approval is essential and that you must be pleased with the final design, but I would like to say here that the form and feeling of the house is, to a great extent, my responsibility, (though the internal details are out of my hands), and I cannot be disinterested in the final result.'

Spence's anger stemmed mainly from his strong dislike of John Colville's design, which he felt could be 'much improved' (Figure 7.6). Although Spence praised the lower portion of the design as 'very good, and quite in keeping with the general feeling of the exterior', he intensely disliked the 'Kissing Birds' which Colville had included in the upper portion. In Spence's opinion they were, 'unscholarly, out of scale, and the form is alien to the material in which they are worked', adding for good measure, 'I think the Council for Art and Industry's axiom of fitness for purpose can be aptly applied here'.[28] Despite Spence's offer to submit an alternative, Colville went ahead with his own design. McDonald and Creswick, an Edinburgh firm of architectural craftsmen, were awarded the contract to make the grilles.

In this way, most of the major changes to the design of Gribloch were made by the Colvilles in consultation with Spence. However, Duncan did make some notable contributions. Perhaps the most significant of these was the addition of an extra chimney on the north elevation. Spence acknowledged this contribution in a letter to Duncan on 14 February 1938: 'I think the introduction of an extra chimney has helped the elevation, but the reason why I had only one chimney was that one approached the house obliquely and I thought that this would be an interesting composition. When I did the sketch however, I was convinced that two chimneys were better.' [29]

Duncan was also responsible for the removal of the fireplace from the south-west wall of the drawing-room to its present location on the north-west wall. (Compare Figures 7.3 and 7.4.) In his letter to John Colville dated 12 January 1938, Duncan wrote that he had made this change as 'it gives you a view of the fireplace upon entering and all the furniture seems to find its place without effort.' [30] This is certainly true. There is no doubt that this subtle change creates a more logical room. It also has the added advantage of keeping the smoke from the chimney away from the swimming-pool. Duncan was probably responsible for the present conventional (and rather dull) chimney-tops. As built, each stack has three chimney-pots on it (Figure 7.1). Spence's original design on the other hand was far more interesting and unusual (Figure 7.3). Each chimney was entirely capped, with side-vents for the smoke. The inspiration for this unusual chimney treatment may once again have been American. A page from a 1930s' issue of *House Beautiful* entitled 'Portfolio of Details: Chimneys', clearly shows this particular design. The author of the article argues that capping the chimney top 'not only acts as a protecting lid but also often improves the draft.' The Colvilles' decision to scrap this design probably resulted from Duncan's criticism of it: 'The treatment of the top of the chimneys gives them a rather thin look, destroying the massive effect I desired from the masonry.' [31]

Duncan's help also appears to have been sought regarding the interior planning of the south-east wing. However, without knowing which set of Spence plans Duncan received, or what alterations (if any) had been made to Spence's early design prior to 'Duncan's Revisions', it is impossible to attribute the changes to Duncan with absolute certainty. One of the most immediately obvious differences between Spence's early plan and the executed one is the change from a circular ante-hall to the present gallery (Figures 7.3 and 7.4). There is no mention of when and why this change was made in the correspondence between Spence and Colville. However, the letter from Duncan to Colville dated 12 January 1938, that accompanied his revised drawings of Gribloch does mention the gallery: 'Opposite the dining room entrance the gallery leads to the Gun and Smoking room which eliminates your going through the cloak room, which I felt an unfortunate necessity.' This statement implies that Duncan may have been responsible for discarding the circular ante-hall in favour of a passage. Duncan continued: 'This gallery is brilliantly lit by the French doors to the garden which balance the doors to the Drawing room.' [32] Whilst a French door leading to the pool was incorporated, the corresponding door on the drawing room side was not.

Despite Spence's annoyance at the Colville's decision to employ Duncan, he did eventually acknowledge his assistance. In a letter to Duncan, dated 14 February 1938, Spence wrote:

> I would like to say here how much I have appreciated your help with regard to
> the internal detailed planning of the house. You may find when you see my plan
> that all your suggestions have not been used, partly because they did not fit in
> with Mr Colville's requirements and partly because they did not lend
> themselves to the external treatment of the house.[33]

As would be expected, Spence was closely involved in the initial discussions concerning
the interior decoration of Gribloch. On 27 June 1938, Spence wrote to Colville that he had
prepared a scheme for the dining-room. He also recommended walnut plywood flooring for
the hall, living-room, drawing- and dining-rooms to give continuity. In the same letter
Spence recommended carpets and tapestries from a firm called Messrs Jeykell who also had
'one of the largest stock of French, Flemish and Eastern fabrics'.[34] In another letter dated
17 November 1938, he referred to perspective drawings of the dining-room, hall and
drawing-room.[35] A scheme for the drawing-room drawn later the same month shows a highly
architectural Georgian Revival panelled room with round-headed china niches, tapestries
and pelmet boxes. Twentieth-century touches include the ornamental radiator screens and
wall sconces fitted with electric candles. The focal point of the scheme was an impressive
carved fireplace, above which hung a bird's-eye view of Gribloch. However, Spence's role
in the interior was drastically curtailed in January 1939 by the appointment of John Hill, of
Green & Abbott Ltd, as interior decorator. A formal letter from Spence to Colville, in which
he varies his terms of contract, reveals that fireplaces, skirtings, architraves and plaster
cornices which 'would have been carried out by us ... are now being carried out by him'
[i.e. John Hill].[36] However, Spence did make some minor contributions. These include the
deep cove mouldings in the bedrooms, Mrs Colville's wardrobe-fitments, the ladies' cloak-
room partition and the plywood flooring in the hall. He also supplied the design for the
dining-room fireplace. In most instances, however, Spence's role was akin to that of Clerk
of Works, executing the Colvilles' wishes, rather than designer.

The choice of Hill as interior decorator for Gribloch may well have been due to Colville's
youngest sister, Georgina. According to Lady Hutchison, Georgina Colville 'had a great
many friends in the art world and was herself quite a good painter'.[37] Seemingly, Hill was a
great friend of hers.

According to Madge Garland, John Hill was 'a striking individualist' who remained un-
touched by the Continental School of interior decoration which 'used new techniques and
materials which permitted novel shapes, and preferred comfort and convenience to display
or nostalgia for the past'. Hill 'was the first to use again light maple-wood furniture, the
first to bring back the deep tones of rich green and plum red which had been in abeyance
for so long and the first to reintroduce patterned wallpapers'.[38] In so doing, John Hill was
one of the first London decorators to reject the strict Functionalism that had been preached
by the likes of Mies van der Rohe and Walter Gropius in the 1920s. He was also one of the
first decorators to combine Regency furniture with Modern interiors. At Gribloch however,

the two styles are confined to separate rooms. The drawing-room and dining-room, for example, are completely traditional in style, with eighteenth-century style fireplaces and furniture. The living-room and entrance-hall, on the other hand, are modern in appearance.

John Hill's design for the living-room was modern, bold and daring (Figure 7.7) with a highly adventurous and sophisticated colour scheme. He used four principal colours – turquoise, aubergine, lime-green and grey. The carpet was purple, the walls grey and the ceiling turquoise. The sofa, matching armchair, Vienna divan and writing chair were all covered in aubergine satin and some were trimmed with specially made turquoise twine fringe. By way of contrast, two other chairs were covered in lime-green satin. A third chair was covered in turquoise-blue mallorde. All four colours were brought together in the hand-stencilled, oyster satin 'Hat and Veil' design curtains. The distinctive stylised feathers which form part of the design had been used in a previous commission by John Hill.[39] Handpainted fabrics were one of Green & Abbot's specialities. Apart from the curtains, Hill also supplied four cushion squares stencilled with a coral ring design. The modern feeling of the room was reinforced by Hill's decision not to have a cornice.[40]

In addition to the soft furnishings, John Hill also designed the architraves, book-alcove and carved wood feather-design light-fitting and fireplace. However, it is clear from the correspondence that the Colvilles played an important part in the design process. A letter to Colville from Hill reveals that Colville had sent his own design-sketch for the living-room fireplace to the decorator and asked him to make a full drawing: 'I am sending you a sketch showing your treatment of the mantelpiece combined with the rounded ingo, which you liked on either side of the chimney breast. I feel that the curves to the mantelpiece do not line up very well with the breaks of the chimney breasts.'[41] The Colvilles may have got their ideas for the living-room fireplace from contemporary American magazines. The executed design is remarkably similar to two illustrations of modern sculptured fireplaces in Mrs Colville's design files. The illustrated fireplace (Figure 7.8) is particularly close to the Gribloch design in that it has a projecting shelf on the right-hand side, with a window immediately adjacent.

A further example of the Colville's possible influence on the decorative treatment of the living-room is the Algernon Newton oil painting of the New York skyline above the mantel-piece. A magazine illustration pasted into Mrs Colville's file shows a modern living-room with a picture of a skyscraper above the fireplace. Significantly, the caption accompanying the picture reads: 'The overmantel decoration depicts a view from the window of a skyscraper, which suggests an American outlook, although this apartment is in the heart of London.' Perhaps the Algernon Newton painting reminded Mrs Colville of her American roots.

The modern decorative treatment of the living-room was complemented by several pieces of furniture by the prominent 1930s designer, Betty Joel. Her company was responsible for John Colville's Australian walnut desk and matching chair, the chrome-and-glass flower-table, the Vienna divan, a nest of drawers and two of the easy chairs.

7.7 The living-room. (*Country Life*)

7.8 Contemporary American magazine illustration showing the fireplaces. (Private Collection)

87)

7.9 The guest bedroom. (*Country Life*)

John Colville's desk appears in an undated Betty Joel catalogue entitled 'Distinctive Furniture For Your Office' (his copy now in the NMRS). According to the accompanying description the desk combined 'distinction and utility with a more elaborate design suited to a private study'.[42] The Colvilles had obviously liked her work for some time since they bought several items for their previous home, Auchengray. The chrome-and-glass flower-table and entrance-hall chandelier, for example, were specially designed for the Colvilles in 1935. The Vienna divan and the easy chairs were purchased at the same time.

According to Isabelle Anscombe, Betty Joel designed furniture 'which was an astute mixture of elements of European Modernism and the luxury of French Art Deco'.[43] Although Joel believed in Functionalism she was no purist. Instead of using plywood for her furniture designs, she chose expensive exotic woods. Moreover, her work reveals a marked preference for unnecessary curves and her Bombay Rosewood bedroom suite at Gribloch (Figure 7.9) is a particularly good example of this. Joel defended her use of curves by arguing that they echoed the Feminine Form.

In summary, it can be said that the scheme evolved by Hill for the living-room, with the assistance of the Colvilles, was very much a room of the Thirties, not the Twenties. It was modern without slavishly toeing the Functionalist line. Moreover, it reveals how it became acceptable once again to design interiors which were bright, bold and fun. This is evidenced by the choice of bright colours, patterned curtains and fanciful circular mirrors and decorative objects.

Before examining John Hill's scheme for the entrance-hall at Gribloch, it is perhaps worthwhile looking at some early proposals for its decoration. Foremost among these must be Nikolaus Pevsner's schemes for the hall and staircase. Although Pevsner is best remembered today as an architectural historian, it is less well known that between 1936–9 he was the chief buyer for Gordon Russell Ltd. It is not known how the Colvilles came into contact with Pevsner. It is possible that John Colville's sister, Georgina, introduced them or that he knew of him through his work for the Scottish Committee for Art and Industry. John Colville may also have been impressed by Pevsner's publications: *Pioneers of Modern Design* (1936) and *An Enquiry Into Industrial Art in England*, which appeared the following year. Pevsner submitted several different design sketches to Colville in May 1938.[44] The letter which accompanied these designs indicates that Pevsner considered 'Sketch One' to be the best solution for the staircase baluster (Figure 7.10). This design featured armour-plated polished glass panels set between dark rose-coloured vertical rails. The hand-rail was also rose-coloured. Pevsner argued that the large expanse of sparkling glass would keep the hall light and airy. Two alternative schemes were suggested for the oval back wall. Both schemes had semi-circular openings towards the dining-room and living-room and two straight-topped niches lined with exotic timber. The major difference between the two designs lay in their treatment of the opening to the ante-hall. Pevsner's first scheme had a round-headed opening. The second was straight-topped with sliding doors, intended to minimise draughts.[45] Although no record as to why Colville rejected Pevsner's schemes has survived, it is reasonable to assume that it was simply because he did not like them.[46]

Interestingly, just five days after Colville had received Pevsner's proposals for the hall and stairway, he wrote to Rowand Anderson, Paul and Partners confirming 'a desire to use glass bricks for the partition between the hall and the ante-hall of the main house … I likewise feel almost certain that the floor of both halls should be made of rubber Terazzo.'[47] Thankfully, Colville's proposal to use glass bricks in the hall was dropped, probably because William Kininmonth (one of Spence's partners) did not feel that it would be wholly satisfactory.[48]

The next person to become involved in the design of the hall was a 'Ferronnier D'Art' from Paris called Raymond Subes. Colville had been impressed by the firm's display of wrought-iron work at the 1937 Paris Exhibition. Subes submitted four different designs for the staircase bannister to Colville between 16 June and 2 August 1938.[49] Colville opted for drawing no. 1484. Subes was not, however, chosen to execute the metal bannister and railing. This was put out to competitive tender. The contract was awarded to Charles Henshaw & Son Ltd, Edinburgh.

John Hill's decorative scheme for the entrance-hall is distinctive and elegant (Figure 7.11). The centre piece of the scheme is the large, oval, hand-knotted rug in shades of mulberry,

7.10 Nikolaus Pevsner (Gordon Russell Ltd), unexecuted design for the entrance hall staircase baluster, wrongly dated 18 May 1936. The sketch accompanied a letter from Spence to Colville dated 18 May 1938. (RCAHMS)

7.11 The entrance hall. (*Country Life*)

blue, white and beige. The design incorporates four shells (two in either corner) intertwined with rope. Sea-gulls fly in amongst them. Hill had used a similar sea-shore theme for an earlier rug design. It featured shells, seaweed and coral in shades of pink, grey, cream, brown and white but was more abstract in style.[50] The maritime theme is continued on the walls where Hill devised a clever shell-and-rope cornice. This was painted white (as were the round-headed niches) to contrast with the blue of the walls and the carpet. The shell-and-rope motif is carried through to the ante-hall, gun-room gallery, first-floor balcony and hall-ways. Furthermore, the round-headed openings to the public rooms were all edged with white plaster rope. Hill was also responsible for the wrought-iron and glass swing door between the ante-hall and front door. Its circular design echoes Subes's staircase bannister. The polished aluminium of the handrail is picked up in Betty Joel's chrome-and-glass chandelier. Appropriate decorative flourishes are provided by two Italian white-painted 'Grotto' chairs and a carved wood leaf light-fitting on the first-floor ceiling. A letter from John Hill to Colville, dated 24 May 1939, proves that the idea for this light-fitting came from an American magazine.[51] These highly decorative objects help give the entrance-hall at Gribloch its distinctive Thirties feel. Clearly, Functionalism played little or no part in Hill's thinking, or that of the Colvilles.

Further indication that the Colvilles probably shared Hill's approach to interior decoration is provided by an article from a May 1933 issue of *House & Garden* entitled 'The New Modernism is assuming an air of elegance'. The article shows an illustration of a fireplace grate which is virtually identical to the one in the master bedroom at Gribloch. The text accompanying this illustration reinforces the move away from the purely Functionalist interiors of the '20s to the desire for something which was less austere but equally modern, elegant and distinctive in the '30s:

> American efforts at modern decoration promise soon to recover from their growing pains. The modernist, having survived the adolescent brutality of 'functionalism', now applies to the more mature qualities of elegance and grace. We have discovered that we can be both modern and comfortable, that we do not have to surround ourselves with objects that outrage the eye or evoke ribaldry, that all our furniture doesn't have to be built in or made of metal tubing. With these notions safely behind us, we can hope that more people will lose their prejudice against a movement that can bring sanity into contemporary decoration.[52]

This quotation could equally be applied to the interiors at Gribloch. The entrance-hall and living-room in particular must be two of the best Scottish examples of this train of thought and taste.

In addition to being excluded from a major role in the interiors, Spence also appears to have been blocked from having any say in the design of the gardens. Spence's initial letters to Colville certainly reveal that he was keen to relate the house to the gardens and the landscape beyond. For example, in a letter to Colville, dated 26 August 1937, Spence wrote:

I have made one big suggestion, that is, that the walled garden should be made part of the house. In this way, I feel our conception will be more up-to-date, and a cohesive whole, the idea being that there should be a gradual stepping down to the pergola, which runs along one wall of the walled garden, and this should be an extremely satisfying feature. I have also incorporated a view terrace, where it would be pleasant to walk when the sun is shining. The suggestion for a swimming pool on the northwest corner of this terrace can be taken for what it is worth, but if the outside wall of the pergola was made of glass, protection from wind would be quite efficient.[53]

None of these suggestions were used.

One of the most unusual and interesting features which was originally proposed for the garden was an outside fireplace. A letter from Spence to Duncan, dated 14 February 1938, reveals that the fireplace was to be on the west side of the house as it was 'a good position to view the sun as it sets over Ben Lomond. It would also close the vista from the walled garden'.[54] In this case however, it seems likely that the inspiration for the fireplace came from the Colvilles, not Spence. In amongst their collection of cuttings there is an article from a 1933 issue of an American magazine entitled 'Autumn Fires Out of Doors'. Nevertheless, it is clear from a letter from Spence to Colville, dated 9 May 1938, that Spence spent a considerable amount of time experimenting and deliberating on the appearance and design of the fireplace: 'I tried balconies, flower boxes, round-headed porticoes in every conceivable shape and the one I enclose herewith is the best of the lot, and I feel reasonably pleased with it.' Spence continued: 'I feel now that you were right in that this fireplace should have a modern tinge about it, and I think my design is modern in flavour.'[55] Spence's drawing reveals that he intended ornamenting the fireplace with a sculpted representation of Pan, the Grecian god of woods and fields. It is not known why the fireplace was not constructed.

The garden was laid out before the house by J. E. Grant White, a garden-architect and landscape consultant based in Chertsey (Surrey), and a founder member of the Institute of Landscape Architects. It would appear that he was commissioned to design the garden in November 1937, since it is known that he made his first site visit at that time.[56] According to Arthur Oswald, the garden 'is designed so as to merge insensibly into the moorland surroundings and on the open sides to form an unobtrusive foreground to the magnificent view'.[57] To the north and west of the house, the lawn soon gives way to moorland heather, blaeberries and rowan trees. This informal theme is continued by a grassed walk-way leading to the walled garden. The walk-way is lined on either side by irregularly-shaped beds filled with cultivated heathers, brooms and azaleas. The walled garden itself is divided into four square sections for fruit, vegetables and flowers, with a small circular pool in the centre. A vinery, fig, nectarine and peach houses are ranged along the south-facing red-sandstone wall. The formality is picked up again nearer the house where a vista was cut through the birch trees on the axis of the hall window and swimming-pool. This gives a lovely view of the Fintry Hills from the staircase window.

It perhaps comes as no surprise that Gribloch bears very little resemblance to Spence's other country houses: Broughton Place near Peebles, Quothquhan near Biggar and the Council for Art and Industry model country house. All four houses were designed and built between 1936 and 1939, but stylistically, they are all different. Although Broughton Place and Quothquhan are both based on seventeenth-century Scottish designs, they look remarkably different, for Broughton Place has a strong vertical emphasis whereas Quothquhan is much lower. Gribloch meanwhile, is a fusion of Regency and Modern architecture. On the other hand, the model country house (which was contemporary with the Gribloch commission) represents a return to the vernacular, with its steeply-sloping, red pantiled roof and skewputts. This more traditional design is all the more intriguing given that it was built at the same time as Spence's uncompromisingly modern ICI Pavilion. Spence's country houses demonstrate his ability to design in a variety of styles. Indeed, William Kininmonth is recorded as saying: 'I suppose we rather prided ourselves on being able to work in any style'.[58]

Nevertheless, Gribloch does display some features which Spence and Kininmonth had utilised in previous and contemporary commissions. Examples include the motif of a semi-circular window extending the full width of the living-room and the use of Crittall metal windows. These features had been used before at three houses in Edinburgh, 'Lismhor' (1932), 4 Easter Belmont Road (1933) and Kininmonth's own house at 46a Dick Place (1934). The interior of the ICI Pavilion had a tight circular entrance-hall with a canti-levered staircase like the one shown in Spence's early Gribloch designs. Quothquhan and 4 Easter Belmont Road also have circular entrance-halls. Kilsyth Academy, in Stirlingshire, (which was sponsored by the Council for Art and Industry) also has a similar staircase window.[59]

Gribloch is a unique Scottish country house. Its distinctive design reflects contemporary attitudes towards architectural and interior design in the Thirties. Twenties Functionalism was beginning to be replaced by an equally modern but less austere approach. It was no longer thought heretical to use architectural elements from previous eras in modern build-ings. This is demonstrated at Gribloch by the use on the exterior of Regency-style bows, wrought-iron balconies and a low-pitched roof treatment on the exterior, and by the com-bination of eighteenth-century and modern decor in the interiors.

Spence proved to be equal to the task set by the Colvilles, to combine the sun and view in the reception rooms, staircase and most of the bedroom suites. This was a difficult prob-lem, but one which Spence persevered with and solved after a great deal of hard work and experimentation. Spence's inverted F-shaped plan is ingenious. It vigorously embraces the landscape and ensures that each of the principal bedrooms has its own spectacular view, so much so that they were later named after the principal mountains to which they look out. Spence was also successful in fusing the Regency and Modern styles into a seamless syn-thesis. Nothing jars the eye or seems out of place. The Colvilles were undoubtedly delighted with their new house. Even at an early stage in the design process, the Colvilles remarked that Spence had struck 'an excellent note' on the outside and the inside was also 'most attractive'.[60]

Given the ambitious scale and complexity of the Gribloch commission, together with the involvement of two architects from different continents, at a time when communications were limited to transatlantic telephone calls and sea-borne mail, the result could have been conceptually weak and lacking in identity. This is not the case. The design is bold, coherent, distinctive and successful. Gribloch is a fitting tribute to the collaboration of the Colvilles and Spence.

National Trust for Scotland

ACKNOWLEDGEMENTS

This article is based on a dissertation I submitted for the MA (Hons) degree in History and History of Art at the University of Edinburgh in 1991. I would like to thank my supervisor, Dr David Howarth, for his continuing encouragement and guidance. I am also grateful for contributions and suggestions from Lady Hutchison, Lady Erskine-Hill, Mr Anthony Blee and my former colleagues at The Royal Commission on the Ancient and Historical Monuments of Scotland.

The author and the AHSS gratefully acknowledge the financial assistance of RCAHMS in the production of this article.

NOTES

Abbreviations

NMRS   The National Monuments Record of Scotland
PC   Private Collection
SRO   Scottish Record Office

1. Candidate's separate statement, dated 4 December 1946 (attached to Spence's application to become a Fellow of the Royal Institute of British Architects, dated 24 December 1946).
2. *The Motherwell Times*, 6 May 1932.
3. Ibid., 28 December 1934.
4. SRO, DD10/299.
5. Anonymous, *Glasgow School of Art through a Century 1840–1940*, 1940, p. 9.
6. *The Glasgow Herald*, 17 April 1937.
7. PC, letter from Duncan to Colville, dated 16 December 1937.
8. PC, draft letter from Mrs Colville to Spence, undated.
9. A. Oswald, 'Gribloch, Kippen, Stirlingshire – 1: The Home of Mr and

Mrs J. M. Colville', *Country Life*, 12 January 1951, pp. 110–14 (p. 110).

10. *The Motherwell Times*, 5 March 1937.

11. PC, letter from Rowand Anderson Paul and Partners to John Colville, dated 16 May 1938.

12. NMRS, DC 14204, dated 7 June 1938.

13. PC, draft letter from Mrs Colville to Spence, undated.

14. PC, Perry Duncan, 'The New Architecture – Simple, Dramatic', extracted from unknown American magazine, undated.

15. PC, copy of letter from Spence to Duncan, dated 14 February 1938.

16. NMRS, Gribloch Collection handlist.

17. NMRS, MS/614/31; *Country Life*, 10 July 1937, p. 27.

18. C. Hussey, 'Joldwynds, Surrey, The Residence of Mr. Wilfrid Greene, K.C.', *Country Life*, 15 September 1934, pp. 276–81 (p. 276).

19. NMRS, MS/614/1/2, dated 26 August 1937.

20. PC, letter from Duncan to Colville, dated 12 January 1938.

21. NMRS, MS/614/1/2, dated 26 August 1937.

22. A letter dated 11 August 1937, from the House Beautiful Reader Service Bureau in New York, states that a copy of the leaflet had been posted to the Colvilles, NMRS, MS/614/8.

23. NMRS, MS/614/4, undated.

24. NMRS, MS/614/5, undated.

25. NMRS, MS/614/1/3, dated 4 October 1937.

26. PC, letter from Spence to Colville, dated 1938.

27. NMRS, MS/614/11/1, dated 14 April 1938.

28. PC, letter from Spence to Colville, dated 6 July 1939.

29. PC, letter from Spence to Duncan, dated 14 February 1938.

30. PC, letter from Duncan to Colville, dated 12 January 1938.

31. NMRS, MS/614/11/1, dated 14 April 1938.

32. PC, letter from Duncan to Colville, dated 12 January 1938.

33. PC, letter from Spence to Duncan, dated 14 February 1938.

34. PC, letter from Spence to Colville, dated 27 June 1938.

35. PC, letter from Spence to Colville, dated 17 November 1938.

36. PC, letter from Spence to Colville, dated 19 January 1939.

37. Letter from Lady Hutchison to the author, dated 27 October 1990.

38. M. Garland, *The Indecisive Decade: The World of Fashion and Entertainment in the Thirties*, London, 1968, pp. 15, 52.

39. S. Calloway, *Twentieth-Century Decoration: The Domestic Interior from 1900 to the Present Day*, London, 1988, plate 318.

40. PC, letter from Hill to Colville, dated 17 January 1939.

41. PC, letter from Hill to Colville, dated 14 February 1939.

42. NMRS, MS/614/23(PR). The same desk design also appears in an office in the days of the 'bright young things' in a book by her husband David Joel, entitled *The Adventure of British Furniture 1851–1951*, London, 1953, p. 214.

43. I. Anscombe, 'Unadorned curves of the feminine form', *The Times*, 16 July 1983.

44. These sketches are now in the possession of NMRS, DC 14166 (PR) – DC 14172 (PR).

45. PC, letter from Pevsner to Colville, dated 19 May 1938.

46. Although Pevsner's work was rejected, he was consulted a year later about the design of the entrance balcony.

47. Copy of letter from Colville to Rowand Anderson Paul and Partners, dated 24 May 1938.

48. PC, letter from Kininmonth to Colville, dated 26 May 1938.

49. NMRS, DC 14159 – DC 14165.

50. Calloway, *Twentieth-Century Decoration*, plate 311.

51. PC, letter from Hill to Colville, dated 24 May 1939.

52. PC, 'The New Modernism is Assuming an Air of Elegance', extracted from an unknown American magazine, May 1933.

53. NMRS, MS/614/1/2, dated 26 August 1937.

54. PC, letter from Spence to Duncan, dated 14 February 1938.

55. PC, letter from Spence to Colville, dated 9 May 1938.

56. PC, statement of professional charges from J. E. Grant White, dated 6 April 1939.

57. A. Oswald, 'Gribloch, Kippen, Stirlingshire', p. 114.

58. C. McKean, *The Scottish Thirties*, Edinburgh, 1987, p. 36.

59. *Scottish Architect and Builders Journal*, November 1938; R. Rennie (ed.), *The Third Statistical Account of Scotland*, Glasgow, 1966, p. 284.

60. NMRS, MS/614/4, undated.

B. T. PENTREATH

Classical Modernism in Fifties Edinburgh: Adam House, by William Kininmonth, 1950–1954

Adam House, the University of Edinburgh's Examinations School in Chambers Street, Edinburgh, was built to the designs of William Kininmonth of the Rowand Anderson Partnership between 1950 and 1954. With a severe 'Adams' façade set against a Festival-style interior and rear elevation, the building provides a fine and unusual example of the spirit of pluralism – mixing contemporary and traditional influences at will – characteristic of much of the best of 1950s British Architecture. In this paper, having introduced the building with an account of its early history, I wish to discuss some of the Scottish influences – both classical and modernist – which informed Kininmonth's design. I shall conclude by arguing that Scottish architectural history owes more attention both to the building and its architect than either have hitherto received.

PROPOSALS FOR A NEW Examinations School for the University of Edinburgh were first mooted shortly after the end of the Second World War and the ensuing election of the Labour Government. In a period of extreme financial stringency, yet one in which the Nation as a whole sought regeneration and renewal, Edinburgh University, with a chronic shortage of accommodation itself, was similarly keen to rebuild and to expand. From the late 1940s the Court and Senatus Papers reveal the first impulses of the massive building programme that was to culminate in Spence's plans for the reconstruction of George Square.

Against these later schemes, the earliest proposals for the new Examination School appear very modest and even insignificant. William Kininmonth, the architect chosen by the University for the work, already enjoyed a position of some importance within the Scottish architectural establishment. During the 1930s, after a training at the Edinburgh College of Art and in London in the Lutyens Office (at that time working on New Delhi), he took up practice, with Basil Spence, in the Rowand Anderson Office at 16 Rutland Square. Together the two men sought to introduce the International Style to Scotland. By the outbreak of war, at which point Spence took the opportunity to break his partnership and move to London, the pair had completed a number of important commissions for town villas and country houses (see, for example, Caroline MacGregor's paper in this volume on Spence's Gribloch).

The file which Kininmonth opened in March 1949,[1] describing the conversion of the Edinburgh Operetta House in Chambers Street into new Examination Rooms, was nonetheless a small affair. By 1 June the scheme had been abandoned, for it was clear that complete rebuilding of the Operetta House (itself the old Gaiety Theatre which had opened in 1875 and which had enjoyed a popular, if not altogether distinguished history) was necessary if the University's requirements were to be met. When, therefore, in April 1949, the possibility arose of the University purchasing the whole site, Kininmonth was instructed to prepare a wholly new scheme five times as expensive as the first.[2] He presented these plans to the Senate on 9 May 1949, writing that

> The following conditions were observed as far as possible in design and planning.
>
> Examination Rooms should be at the rear of the building with staircases at the front, thus minimising traffic noises.
>
> Floor levels above the ground floor should approximate to floor levels of adjoining buildings with a view to possible future extensions.
>
> Owing to the depth of the site, artificial lighting, heating and ventilation cannot be avoided but the maximum natural lighting should be contrived.

In short, within the brief laid down by the University, exactly what we might expect. The arrangement of the accommodation as built (Figure 8.1) seems largely fixed: five stories, including a basement, with entrance halls at the front and examination halls to the rear, stairs to either side and a seating capacity for 1,007 students. Crucially, however, Kininmonth continues:

> The character of the building should be contemporary. The facade to Chambers Street should be simple and direct with a scale and breadth to correspond with the Old University buildings opposite ...
>
> It is hoped that in order to offset the extreme simplicity of the design it may be possible to introduce a high quality finish in the Entrance Hall, staircases and facade to Chambers Street.[3]

The building was to be cast in steel reinforced concrete with hung ceilings. Externally, it would be finished with brick walls with stone and artificial stone facing; internally with linoleum and 'acotile' flooring, plasterboard walls, hoptonwood stone and terazzo detailing, aluminium or bronze windows and internal metal folding screens.

Extensive searches in the Rowand Anderson Office and in the University archive have failed to reveal any drawings for this scheme, and I believe it unlikely that any will now emerge. Within a study of context, however, it is possible to determine the essential qualities of the design. First, of course, Kininmonth makes plain the basic nature of the building when he describes the 'extreme simplicity' that he seeks. Second, the materials which he proposes place the building firmly within a well-established modernist architectural vocabulary; and, finally, it is easy to place such a scheme within Kininmonth's own oeuvre – buildings such as the Renfrew Airport terminal which, with a clear debt both to Le Corbusier and to Perret, was rising contemporary with Adam House.[4] In the spring of 1950, Kininmonth submitted plans to the Town Authorities, amongst which was a sketch elevation, now lost, whose roof was to be of copper, walls constructed with a steel framed structure faced with stone slabs

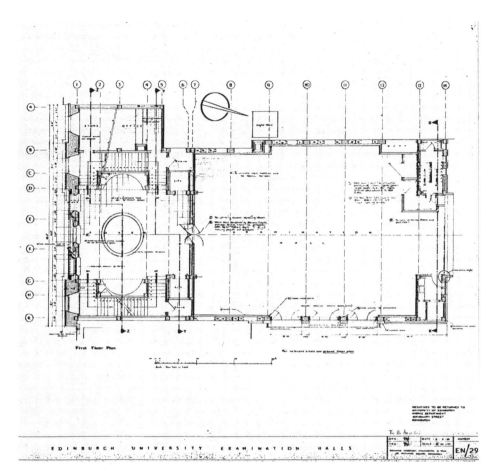

8.1 William Kininmonth, Adam House, 1950–4, ground-floor plan. (University of Edinburgh)

and a granite plinth and with Crittal window surrounds in bronze.[5] At the same time he wrote to the University thanking the Court for its continuing support, concluding with his belief that planning approval 'will be given although we may experience some difficulty in the initial stages'.[6]

In the event such confidence was misplaced. On 15 May he wrote to the Town Planning Officer that 'it is most unlikely that the final design of the elevation will correspond with the sketch sent to you recently, as the latter was submitted *merely to show that the building might rise above cornice level*'[7] (my emphasis): hardly the language of a confident planning application; and at some stage in the following two weeks the modernist proposal was abandoned. On 30 May Kininmonth received a message from the Principal, Sir Edward Appleton, commending a new design, and the next day he submitted these proposals to the Planning Department for approval. Accompanying the scheme, he wrote:

If the site is examined in relation to its surroundings it will be seen that the architectural atmosphere of the street as a whole is overpoweringly classic and it is extremely doubtful if on this particular site with the University buildings opposite any other form of architecture would look comfortable and in scale with its surroundings, and I was forced to the conclusion that the new building should:

Conform in its architecture to the architecture of the street in which every other building is in the classic tradition.

It should link with the buildings on either side and so retain the architectural unity of the existing block.

It should be an obvious part of the Old University, and

It should be designed as far as possible as part of a 'Gateway' to the east end of Chambers Street with the projecting and pedimented portion of the Old University forming the other part and together framing the street scene.[8]

Both the language and basic architectural concerns now being expressed are new, but if, as such, it is important to understand why the design underwent such radical alteration, I am unable to present any conclusive evidence to that end. The office files are reticent as to who was responsible, the Senate and Court papers are typically silent, while the Planning Department destroys all correspondence concerning rejected applications. Objections from the planning committee or from University patrons – both potential conservative critics of a modernist scheme – seem less likely in the light of the confidence which both had at one time or another expressed in the earlier design.[9] The Cockburn Association may have objected but I have found no evidence to suggest this. Elsewhere,[10] it has been proposed that Robert Matthew, Kininmonth's friend and contemporary, found the Modernist design unsuitable for the Chambers Street site, but 'given [Matthew's] later determination to destroy George Square, and his uncompromising Midlothian County Offices, which are surely in a much more important position in relation to historic buildings than is Chambers Street,'[11] this is unlikely. In short, in the absence of evidence to the contrary, we must conclude that the decision was Kininmonth's, and that it was made to address his stated concerns for harmony and propriety within the streetscape, qualities perhaps lacking in the 'direct simplicity' of the earlier programme.

This limited account of the early history of Adam House serves to introduce the wider themes of traditionalist and modernist thought that run parallel through the building. For while the façade to Chambers Street (Figure 8.2) provides a witty, if somewhat severe, re-interpretation of the Adam style and of Old College opposite, even a cursory glance at the interior (Figure 8.3) or the rear elevation, hidden down a narrow Close off Guthrie Street (Figure 8.4), reveals the strongly modernist idiom that Kininmonth here chose to maintain from the first scheme. In so saying, it is possible to detect a number of influences, various and often contradictory, which play upon the design and which, within the limits of this paper, it is my purpose to discuss here.

8.2 Adam House, Chambers Street façade. (Author)

8.3 Adam House, general view of the interior, *Evening News*, 18 May 1955. (Scotsman Publications)

I have mentioned above Kininmonth's position, with Spence, as one of the principle exponents of the International Modern Movement in Scotland. Of the two, there can be no doubt that Spence was considered by contemporaries to be the more brilliant: 'here', they were led to believe, 'could be Scotland's leading modernist'.[12] The partnership nonetheless indicates Kininmonth's facility as a modernist. His own house at 46a Dick Place, Edinburgh, shows a skilful assimilation of the vocabulary of white rendered walls, of contrast between the curve and the rectangle and of flat, interconnecting roof terraces that characterises the international style in England.[13] Two years later the same themes were re-interpreted on a larger scale at Lismhor, on the Easter Belmont Road, where Kininmonth worked in partnership with Spence. Together, according to John Gifford, the two buildings introduce the Modern Movement to Scotland.[14]

If this is the case, then Adam House, particularly its interior and to some extent its rear elevation, can be placed within the tradition established by Kininmonth at Dick Place and Lismhor. Though the three buildings have very different functional concerns, the Adam House interior shares an architectural vocabulary, concerned with qualities of space, light and the interplay of geometric form, with the 1930s villas. On a formal level, there is an affinity between the contrast of 'curve and rectangle' which McKean recognises at Dick

8.4 Adam House, general view of the rear elevation. (Author)

Place[15] and the relationship between circle and square which characterises the architectural language at Adam House. When, in 1927, Frederick Etchells translated Le Corbusier's *Vers Une Architecture*, with its 'hymning of the great primary forms of cube, cone, sphere, cylinder and pyramid, and ... its memorable dicta "Architecture is the masterly, correct and magnificent play of masses brought together in light"',[16] he introduced many of the themes that in a different context, and albeit in a changed architectural language, were to be touched upon in the interior configuration of Adam House.

The 1930s work is equally indicative of the stylistic ambivalence which we have identified at Adam House. Lismhor was amongst the last of the emphatically 'modern' houses carried out by the Kininmonth-Spence practice, and though this has given rise to the notion of Spence as 'an unfulfilled modern genius suffocated between the slump and World War II',[17] McKean is right to suggest alternative reasons for the break.[18] On the one hand, 'of the many houses designed by Spence in the 1930s, only the first (that is, Lismhor) had a flat roof, and it failed':[19] and on the other, both Kininmonth and Spence display a notable adherence to vernacular forms: though 'modern in the sense of planning and detail', writes McKean, 'these houses are nonetheless very Scots: great pitched roofs, white harling, and horizontal glazing ... Spence shared some of that seeking after native roots for modernism that was motivating Hurd, Reiach, Mears, Lindsay, Mansfield Forbes, Sir John Stirling Maxwell et al.'.[20] Thus, Spence's belief that

> our tradition is really a sensitive reaction to existing conditions, and the
> production of a building that is fitted for its purpose, direct and simple in its
> conception, with an eye for proportion, and the understanding use of materials
> ... the judicious selection of forms during the Renaissance and Regency
> periods proves that old forms adapted to conditions that are suitable for their
> use is a sound policy[21]

can be related not only to his neo-vernacular modernist experiments but, in a different context, to Kininmonth's language at Adam House: concern for streetscape, harmony, propriety, and the adaption of 'old forms to conditions suitable for their use'. By the 1950s, transmuted by the post-war regeneration programme, such concerns had emerged across the wider field of British architecture in so-called 'Festival Style'; which, as Alan Powers has recently argued, emerged directly out of the pre-war work of the MARS Group and their modernist contemporaries.[22]

Alongside these aspects of the building, however, and the essential distinguishing feature of the second design, is the rigorously classical façade of dressed Hewarthburn stone. Arranged on a tripartite system and with a grand Serlian-derived window at the *piano nobile*, the façade, according to Kininmonth, was designed 'to harmonise with the street scene, where all buildings are classical in conception, as an obvious part of the old university opposite and as a tribute to Robert Adam and his family'.[23]

With these words, Kininmonth introduces the three basic concerns which went to inform the second design for Adam House. Adam architecture self-evidently proved crucial in formulating the design. Not only were the new Examination Halls to stand directly opposite Old College, but, as Kininmonth wrote to Charles Stewart, the University Secretary in 1954:

> I have been able to verify my information that the family home of the brothers Adam stood on the site of the new buildings. The print in the University Library, illustrating the ceremony at the laying of the Foundation Stone of the University, shows that it was a fairly large villa standing in its own grounds and fronting on to Adam Square, an open space at the east end of what is now Chamber [*sic*] Street. I understood the building once housed the Watt Institution, now the Heriot-Watt College, and was probably taken down when Chamber Street was built.
>
> I think, therefore, that it would be a very happy inspiration to call the new buildings 'Adam House', and if this has been finally agreed I shall have the inscription cut when I hear from you.[24]

Notwithstanding these sentiments, it is important that nowhere in the early stages of the design does Kininmonth refer to the Adams or to Adam Square. In the first Modernist proposal, he talks only of 'the old University buildings opposite'.[25] and even in the letter accompanying the traditional scheme of 1950, Adam is not mentioned. A letter of 23 June 1950 explaining this design to the Assistant Secretary of the University (where we might especially expect to find reference to Old College and its architect) repeats his concerns for harmony and conformity, but similarly does not mention the Adams. Indeed, within the files, Kininmonth's first reference to the connection is made as late as 25 October 1954.[26] The letter is illuminating not least because it confirms, even at this late date, that a name for the new halls had not been established. In the absence of evidence to the contrary, it may be asked whether Kininmonth's specific references to Adam are retrospective, used only to give the building meaning after the event.

Such a conclusion ignores, however, the weight of visual evidence suggesting a vital Adam influence, above all of the Adam townhouse. Kininmonth describes [see above] the print of the Old College foundation stone ceremony, and this, with a nineteenth-century wood-engraving of the 'Watt Institution and School of Arts, Adam Square' (Figure 8.5), makes plain the architectural character of the building. Central – both in position and importance – is a large Serlian window, and when it reappears at the Examination Halls, transfigured, certainly, but in the same central position, we must conclude that Kininmonth is making a direct quotation. His belief that the new Examination Halls stood on the site of the Adam Townhouse was confirmed as early as July 1950, several months before building work started (and before, therefore, the design had reached conclusion), when demolition of the Operetta House revealed the stone well which stood in the garden and provided the original water supply of the old villa.[27]

In a subsequent analysis of the principles governing the proportions of the façade, Kininmonth introduced a further reference to Adam architecture when he wrote that

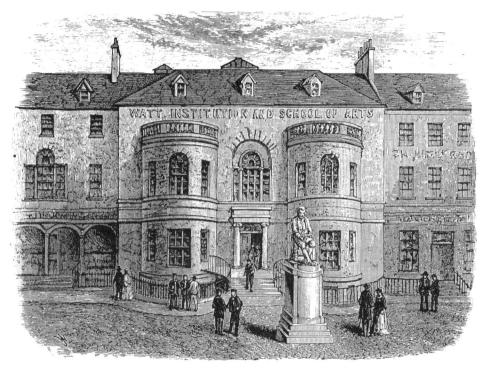

8.5 The Watt Institution and School of Arts, Adam Square. (*Grant's Old and New Edinburgh*)

> Some attempt was also made within the purer theory [of] mathematical proportion to include a more emotional symbolism. The general conception is that of a triumphal arch through which all students pass to success or failure. The pedimented treatment of the facade was adopted in the first instance to echo the pediment of the Old University on the opposite side of Chambers Street and thus create a visual 'gateway' within the street, while the arch was intended to provide a mutual association with the 'Old Quad' in the minds of Students and the general public.[28]

We might question the extent to which the passing public or the soon-to-be-examined student notice the finer points of such emotive symbolism, but the evidence is of a clearly-stated architectural debt. It is interesting to note that the three volume Thezard edition of *The Works in Architecture of Robert and James Adam* was amongst Kininmonth's collection of books sold at his death.[29] As regards the façade at least, we may conclude that the Adam influence, and particularly the example of the villa itself, played strongly in the creation of Adam House.

Alongside the two influences which I have discussed here – both Kininmonth's 1930s work with Spence and the late eighteenth-century neoclassicism of Robert Adam and his family – there are, of course, other characteristics which run equally strongly in the building: we

8.6 Adam House, general view of the façade from Chambers Street. (Author)

could quote the architecture of Eric Gunnar Asplund and the Swedish pluralists on the one hand, or of Lutyens and Soane on the other, not to mention the wider culture of 'Festival Style' as a whole. In choosing to concentrate on these two, particularly Scottish elements, we nonetheless highlight the peculiar mix of traditional and contemporary, classical and modernist, which makes Adam House such an interesting exemplar of its period. Within the traditional scheme of British architectural history, which has perhaps sought to identify a series of steadily-changing, but, within themselves, unified architectural styles,[30] Kininmonth might be seen as somewhat suspect for employing different languages alongside one another at Adam House. But the very meaning of the Examination Hall was contradictory, or at least complex:

> Architecturally, the building is intended as a visual reminder, that, in addition to its principal function which is to equip its graduates for their life in the contemporary world, the University is also a storehouse of ancient learning, much of which is valuable in any age.[31]

Only when Kininmonth had embraced a stylistic dichotomy – what I have called in my introduction a pluralist approach – was he able to develop the building to such ends. Adam House, though lingering in a state of wilful neglect, is a fine building: for the historian, one of tremendous interest, and, I believe, some importance. Its architect, nonetheless, has met with scant regard and much misunderstanding. To my knowledge no research has been made into the building beyond that which I present here. The building seems never to have been illustrated in the architectural press, while the *Buildings of Scotland Edinburgh* volume dismisses Adam House with a single, terse line: 'the name', it writes, 'is not a sick joke but [commemorates] Adam Square'.[32]

Few of Kininmonth's contemporaries, either in Scotland or in England, sought to handle stone, classical architecture so wittily or so well, and fewer still achieved such a modest and elegant approach to the problem of placing a modern building in a historic streetscape (Figure 8.6). I believe that Adam House provides, of its period, an exemplar of the best of what this Society seeks in the practice of architecture today. Its architect, we may conclude, should be celebrated for his honesty in recognising the limits of a one-style-at-a-time approach, although so far he has received only misunderstanding, and relegation to the second rate.

ACKNOWLEDGEMENTS

This paper is derived largely from my dissertation *Adam House and its Architectural Influences*, presented for the MA (Hons) degree in the History of Art at Edinburgh University (1994) [copy in the NMRS]. I should like to thank my supervising tutors, Dr David Howarth and John Lowrey, for their help in its preparation, together with Richard Ewing, Ian Gow, Alan Powers and several others for their assistance.

NOTES

1. Complete office files pertaining to the work at Adam House are held in the Rowand Anderson Partnership offices at 16 Rutland Square, Edinburgh. I should like to extend particular thanks to Richard Ewing for kindly allowing me full access to these.

2. The cost of the initial conversion scheme was estimated at £35,000. On 26 May 1949 an estimate for the new plans was received for £175,000. This gives some indication of the relatively modest nature of the first proposal.

3. Letter, 9 May 1949, William Kininmonth (WHK) to Charles Stewart (CHS), University Secretary.

4. The hyperbolic arch of the Renfrew Airport building (1951–3), for example, was based on the Corbusier competition entry for the Palace of the Soviets, Moscow, 1931. Kininmonth also expressed admiration for Auguste Perret, and especially for the Church of Notre Dame at Le Raincy, 1922–3. See Lawrence Wodehouse, 'Old Guard, Avant-Guarde', *Building Design*, 23 February 1979, p. 29.

5. Letter, 4 April 1950, WHK to Town Planning Department.

6. Letter, 23 November 1949, WHK to Assistant Secretary, Edinburgh University.

7. Letter, 15 May 1950, WHK to D. M. Plumstead, Town Planning Officer.

8. Letter, 31 May 1950, WHK to Town Planning Clerk.

9. See Edinburgh University Court, *Signed Minutes*, vol. 20, p. 539: 'the committee were strongly in favour of this proposal'. Letter, 16 May 1950, WHK to CHS: 'Mr Plumstead telephoned me this morning when he explained that the committee does not object to the *design* of the proposed Exam. Halls.'

10. Interview with Richard Ewing, 20 February 1994.

11. My thanks to Oliver Barratt for his thoughts on the likelihood of Robert Matthew as an influence in the change of design, quoted from a letter to the author, 27 February 1994.

12. C. McKean, *The Scottish Thirties: An Architectural Introduction*, Edinburgh, 1987, p. 36.

13. L. Wodehouse, 'Old Guard', argues that Kininmonth's use of the dominant semi-circular drawing-room window may, indeed, have influenced English international style developments, such as the Connel, Ward and Lucas House at Moor Park, Hertfordshire (1936–7). Nonetheless, a building such as Mendelsohn and Chermayeff's De La Warr Pavilion at Bexhill-on-Sea (1934–5), which employs a similar motif, did prefigure the publication of the Kininmonth and King Houses in the architectural press in 1935.

14. J. Gifford, C. McWilliam, and D. Walker, *The Buildings of Scotland: Edinburgh*, Harmondsworth, 1984, p. 65.

15. C. McKean, *Edinburgh: An Illustrated Architectural Guide*, Edinburgh, 1983, cat. 314.

16. D. Dean, *The Thirties: Recalling the English Architectural Scene*, London, 1983, p. 14.

17. C. McKean, *The Scottish Thirties*, p. 36.

18. Having said this, we should remember, as Wodehouse argues, that Spence was searching for clients who would commission a modern building throughout the 1930s. Dr John King, who commissioned Lismhor, was without doubt an unusual client in Edinburgh of the early 1930s.

19. C. McKean, *The Scottish Thirties*, p. 36.

20. Ibid.

21. B. Spence, *Building Industries*, April 1938.

22. A. Powers, 'The Reconditioned Eye: Architects and Artists in English Modernism', *AA files*, no. 25, 1993.

23. WHK, notes on *Adam House*, 1955.

24. Letter, 24 November 1954, WHK to CHS.

25. Letter, 23 November 1949, WHK to CHS.

26. Letter, 25 October 1954, WHK to CHS.

27. Letter, 24 November 1954, WHK to CHS.

28. WHK, notes to *Adam House*, 1957.

29. Phillips, George Street, Edinburgh, catalogue of *Printed Books, Maps, Postcards and Prints*, for sale at Auction, 7 June 1989, cat. no. 35. Kininmonth's library was disposed of in this sale.

30. See, for example, J. Summerson, *Architecture in Britain 1530–1830*, Harmondsworth, 1953, ch. 21, 'The Individual Contribution of James Gibbs', pp. 209–14.

31. WHK, notes to *Adam House*, 1955.

32. J. Gifford et al., *The Buildings of Scotland*, p. 223.

The Fourth Colin McWilliam Memorial Lecture: Living with an Eye

Colin McWilliam.

There is a pun in the title of this lecture that is wholly inapplicable to anything to do with my father, Colin McWilliam. To the reader, it may not be visible, but you, as listeners, will hear it at once. The title I chose was 'Living with an Eye'. I thought it expressed something of the informed vigilance of my father's approach to his life and his work, which were inseparable from one another. He was never on holiday from his enthusiasms and convictions. In that he was a very overworked, but also a blessed, man.

In this way he had the unconfined commitment of an artist, but how unlike the popular idea of the artist, 'temperamental', demanding, showy, he was, too. For, I realised, the title could sound as though I were going to talk to you tonight about 'Living with an "I"': capital I, not E. Y. E. My father was almost ridiculously without ego as it is understood in the world, and especially today's world, with its emphasis on psychiatry and selfhood, a world whose rapacity and concentration on destructive competition and gain at all costs he so deplored that it was on this subject that the only moments occurred when I can recall my father actually approaching being boring.

This constant theme was not the complaining of a person who simply perceives deterioration because he is getting older. Apart from physically – and he was always in bad health, and took no care of himself – he hardly got older. He never settled into opinions, respected appearances without substance, compromised, or became pompous. He hadn't developed the persona behind which so many adults hide, deploying it to impress and hector. He was not threatened by the young. Least of all did he, as people are held to do, become more conservative as he grew older. 'If I thought,' he said to listeners to Radio Scotland in Jubilee Year, 1977, 'as many people think, that everything has gone hopelessly wrong, then I might as well stop talking and play you some soothing music.'

Here tonight, you will not need to be told that conservation is not conservative, in the retrograde sense that has come to be known derogatorily as 'theme parking'. The jellified past of 'heritage', that is relentlessly marketed in every medium, is everything my father was innocent of; to do with materialism, aspiration, the accumulation of goods, lifestyle, it is a disease afflicting the artistic and cultural life of England and Scotland alike. Lazy thinking and the constant appetite for more Aunt Sallies to fill the disgraceful 'style' sections of our newspapers have somehow come to ally conservation with ossified touristic daintiness. It is plain from reading what my father wrote that his impulse to conserve was never separated from an impulse that one might, if it did not sound horribly pi, call both practical and moral. Use, beauty and history were what he looked for in a building, and he was clear about the worth of the last quality. 'What does it matter, one might ask?', he wrote. 'The answer is that in any age, but especially in one where change and even alienation prevail, it is pleasant to find connections in life-connections between present and past, knowledge and experience.' He put it even more explicitly in a lecture entitled 'Working Together in Conservation': 'Links between things, links between ideas and people, are what we are here to talk about'.

The separation of the idea of conservation from the idea of use is a deep and meretricious severance promoted by people preoccupied by surface without any supporting structural armature. Very often it has not occurred to them that in order to look good a structure must work well, because, as my father was well aware, people are not educated to understand with their eyes. There is a need for education such as that encouraged by the memorial fund set up in his memory, not merely for young people who are set on becoming architects or architectural historians, though that *is* essential, but also for those who are to be citizens at ease with their past and their country's, thus establishing a coherent ground for the future, both civic and moral. Here he is on his notion of a visual education: 'Visual education, which is certainly necessary, needs a very careful definition indeed. At present [18 January 1972] it is almost entirely political, telling us what we ought to like, how to get good marks in a design exam we shall never take. The first aim of visual education must be the removal of cant. The second must be to forget visual matters and look at what makes things work. And the third is just to look at things in honest visual terms, identifying what we enjoy and what we don't. Only with this sort of background, if we are going into the education business at all, can we expect people choosing paint colours for front doors, designing motorway bridges, siting factories in the countryside, to make decisions which in turn will make sense. And what more do we want?'

I don't think I ever heard my father use the words moral or immoral. He was not a prig, and had not a gossipy nature, so I'm sure he would have been chary, in spite of being by adoption a citizen of this beautiful, gossipy, city, of judging other people. But his understanding of architecture, most particularly the layout and architecture of towns, seems to me, when I read it, and when I recall his various crusades – it's not an exaggeration to call them that – about threatened buildings, streets or squares, to be a moral understanding. Here he is writing in *Scottish Townscape*, published in 1975: 'The awkward, or convenient, fact that people will eventually become visually accustomed to anything that does its job moderately well is another reason for guarding rather than relaxing the accepted usages of townscape.' I would like to set beside this some words from the Heriot-Watt bulletin that state his central conviction: 'Conservation accounts for about half the work of the small or medium-size architectural firms in Britain. To do it well requires an understanding of traditional design and building practice. And, incidentally, this understanding is directly relevant to the making of new architecture. Yesterday's buildings are *test cases* from which tomorrow's can benefit.' My father never wanted to live in a world preserved in aspic. He welcomed the modern, so long as it learned from the past, from its mistakes as much as its triumphs, without slavishly imitating it.

This open-eyed and open-minded attitude seems ever harder to sustain in a profession that appears, even to a layman like me, to be riven with schism almost as harmfully as the contemporary church. Typically, forgivingly, my father described this condition among architects often in his writings, calling it 'self-doubt'. Modernism and classicism seem, in much of the new work that is going up today, to have turned their faces away from one another in a manner that can have only sterile issue. The professionals disagree while the public is increasingly baffled about the environment in which we are asked to live. Nostalgias flourish that could not, in the early days of urban slash and burn, have been anticipated; we miss streets, intimacy, claustrophobia almost. This does not mean we need puristically to hanker for outside sanitation and the good old Friday night beating. Conservation has become confused in the minds of many with re-creation So parodic is our society, we understand the past not through its real manifestations but through a wholly modern and artificial, got-up, 'realism', that makes of the past a great dead still life sprayed with odours of decay made by master perfumers for huge industrial agglomerates. A visit to the – shamefully enjoyable, thoroughly camp – *Yorvik* or *Oxford Story* will tell you more quickly than I could in words what will be the conclusion of re-creation without imagination. The end result is that those who have access to and understanding of the artefacts and buildings of the past feel superior to those, many more, who enjoy and absorb – and believe – the 'new past'. The divisiveness, even cynicism, of this increasingly popular course of 'infotainment' comes perilously to resemble an aesthetic branch of social engineering.

Of course such slippages of understanding between the times have always been part of intellectual history and critical fashion. Perhaps because we are more in number and have more information more quickly than ever before, we need quick ways of understanding what has taken many centuries to evolve. With the human love of coming to the fast and wrong conclusion and sticking to it, in order to feel ourselves to be strong-minded, we seem to have grafted the idea of conservation onto the deep-rooted weed of national nostalgia, that spreads uncontrollably when a nation's self-esteem is low. Then the ignorant, the snobs and the more barren purists feel justified in dismissing conservation, saying it's without energy, decadent, backward looking. Imagine if anatomists started saying such things about the structure and function of the body: 'No, eyes have been round the front too many millennia now. It's time we tried them up in the hairline, like dormers.'

In *Scottish Townscape*, my father discusses with his usual relaxed wit the moral indignation of the language of the Victorians, notably their most influential critic of architecture, Ruskin, faced with Georgian Edinburgh:

> John Ruskin was a professed anti-Georgian, and the second half of the nineteenth century was pervaded by his seductive blend of aesthetic and moral judgement. He sanctified the bay window and the pointed arch, the leafy capital fresh from the craftsman's chisel, and in a curiously unreal way he sought to connect architecture and life. He hated the plain, flat-headed Georgian windows that in his view so lamentably failed to express this connection, and actually made a count of them on his way along Picardy Place, York Place and Queen Street to deliver the first of his four *Lectures on Art and Architecture* in Edinburgh on a November evening in 1853; the total was 678, and nothing has since happened to alter it.

Here I must interrupt to say that it is a November evening almost twenty years after my father was writing that, and over a hundred and forty years after Ruskin gave his lecture and I'm afraid that I have not counted the flat-headed windows as I came, but I hope they remain 678 in number. Let me continue with this excerpt from *Scottish Townscape*, because it exemplifies a combination of alertness and laissez-faire that characterised my father:

> [Ruskin's] ideas, including what amounted to a programme for gothicising Georgian Edinburgh, were not very warmly received. But his bigotry lived on, and the twentieth century condemned Victorian architecture in the moral terms it had learned from this most popular – and in some ways most influential – of Victorian critics. George Scott-Moncrieff ends his book *Edinburgh* (it is otherwise an exemplary study of the city and its buildings) with some nicely aimed but ill-conceived pot-shots like this one:
>
> > After William Burn came David Bryce, and with him Scottish architecture

plumbed the depths of meaningless ostentation, derivation in which every source is arrogantly misunderstood. Most of Bryce's work was done at country seats, where he ruined many a fine old castle, and not infrequently its fine old family as well. However, in 1868–70 he reconstructed the Bank of Scotland on its prominent site at the top of the Mound … when Bryce had finished with it everything about it was bad, and it remains to this day a hideous conglomeration of architectural fatuity.

My father continues, in his own words now:

Nobody who has seen [the Bank] and Bryce's other bank buildings in Edinburgh, or visited the country houses which he was commissioned to restore or extend (from Blair Castle and Cullen House to Robert Adam's Newliston) will take this knockabout comment very seriously. Yet now that not merely the reputation but the survival of a building may hang on a critic's word, such sweeping generalisations are dangerous.

This passage contains many of my father's traits. It is funny – I am quite sure he, unlike his idle elder daughter, counted those windows. It is written in precise, poetically apt language ('the leafy capital fresh from the craftsman's chisel'). It is generous. It takes a long view. It is informed and unostentatious. It is very polite to the reader. He always assumed one did, rather than did not, know things; the effect of this was to make one go and find those things out, and try to learn more. This trust in the pupil, or junior, or, in my own case, child, must have been part of his effectiveness as a teacher. As a writer, he is clear, elegant, unstrained in tone and unafraid of using the vernacular, or indeed the eccentric, word, if it is the right one. Throughout his architectural descriptions, in whichever book or article they are to be found, runs the strong natural ability to describe what he saw, absolutely directly, so that it is recreated in the mind of the reader. It is as hard to do this as it is to draw buildings – which he could also do; I hope it will not be taken as filial piety only if I say that I think he could do something even harder. In the describing or drawing of the building, he could make one see it not only as it was but also as he saw it, because his style was, without over-flavouring or affectation, quite his own. This style informs even his more technical writings, such as the *Edinburgh* volume in The Buildings of Scotland series, on which he collaborated with John Gifford, David Walker and Christopher Wilson.

His description of the monuments in the Greyfriars Kirkyard is full of a gentle, perfectly reverent funpoking, that I do not think will have prejudiced his new companions there against him, even though he called one memorial cherub 'pudgy' and notices some lions flanking an aedicule erected to James Murray of Deuchar (1650), with their mouths 'stuffed with drapery'. The richness, variety and dignity of these monuments to great Scots, the frequent references to Italy in their style and the delicate balance between splendour and frailty, loss and humour that characterise monumental art, seem perfectly to fit out the place where my father is now. He is not the only person there whose memorial tablet nods to Vitruvius. Another stone lion (I think Daddy liked cats) holds a panel that says:

> Great artisan, grave senator, JOHN MILNE
> Renown'd for learning, prudence, parts, and skill,
> Who in his life Vitruvius' art had shown,
> Adorning others' monuments: his own
> Can have no other beauty, than his name,
> His memory and everlasting fame.

As it happens, it was not, either in life or in architecture, splendour but well-madeness, if there is such a word, that inspired my father. He himself was modest – and evasive about his attainments – both by nature and by upbringing. His mother was the most determinedly quiet person I have ever known. He mistrusted flashiness, perhaps because it distracts from substance, more likely, I suspect, because there is, or can be something unkind about it. He was fond of the rather melancholy vulgarity of Blackpool; we went there together once and had a horrible time in something called The Fun House. That is the earliest use I can remember of 'fun' being used as an adjective; it was 1963. It wasn't just an adjective; it was a lie. My father got an electric shock from the tail of a papier maché elephant with a spring-loaded trunk-extensor facility. By night the trams turned into ships of light and space rockets and the trip was saved, and I was hooked too. More than having no taste for luxury, I think he had even a distaste for it, as the world sees it. His luxuries were opera, looking at things (which was also his life; without it he would have starved away), and talking to strangers. I'll come to that later.

Something of my father's passion for the little, the ignored, comes through in a passage of Cobbett, who visited Edinburgh in the course of his tour in 1832, which my father quotes in *Scottish Townscape*:

> I think little of [Edinburgh's] streets and rows of houses, though all built of stone, and though everything in LONDON and BATH is beggary to these; I think nothing of Holyroodhouse; but I think a great deal of the fine and well ordered streets of shops; of the regularity which you perceive everywhere in the management of business; and I think still more of the absence of all that foppishness, and that insolent assumption of superiority, which you meet with in the fashionable parts of the great towns in England.

I must stress at this point that my father was nothing so simple as an inverted snob. Edinburgh, with its palatial streets actually composed of apartments and flats and businesses, and built to be so composed, can stand as a good metaphor for his sense of the democracy of the visual world.

Which brings me to the title of my lecture. Why have I taken so long to get to the point? Not only because I'm my father's daughter and McWilliams are evasive – as well as being dedicated mutterers and slippers-off-into-another-room. The more serious reason why I've staved off talking to you this evening about my father, perforce as I knew him, is that I am sure that many of you knew him, or at any rate his professional self, much better than I did. Many of you will have memories less clouded by passed time. Those of you who were his colleagues or students will have much to tell me. All I can do is to give some notion of what it was like to be his child, and my half-sister Anna has followed more closely in his pro-fessional footsteps than I *and* was taught by him. I think the only reason I can be here is that the oldest always has to jump first.

I have to come clean. I hated and resented buildings. The reasons for this will be obvious to you. They were my rivals. Actually, they were not even that; they were supreme in our house. There are even people here tonight whom I connected so intimately with buildings that I longed for them to be off when they came to our house in Warriston Crescent. I'm not sure when the tide turned, but I think it must have been at a much younger age than I realised, for I remember with relish the restoration of the fishing villages of Fife, Crail, Pittenweem, Anstruther, and of Culross, and the ferry journey we'd to take over to these towns in those days before the Forth Road Bridge was built. I remember sitting next to my father while he drew with his Flomaster or orange pencils with black leads, on tracing paper, or on those pads you've to slice like a white loaf to get off the drawing. He smoked noisily, as though it was essential to his breathing, all the time he drew. There are a few black and white photographs – pronounced, some of you will recall, with an Audenesque short *a* by my father – from this time. My father, in his early thirties, looks about seventeen. He was very thoughtful to my bear who was older than he and therefore often ousted him from the – rare – available, comfortable perch. The technical terms interested me. 'Harling' and 'pepperpot' were the first, followed by 'astragal'. My father did not talk down. He was not whimsical. He described things as they were, and this was preferable to the winsome fictions that some adults habitually employ with children. At Crathes and at the Binns, where the Dalziels' pug dog had a tail like twisted roll and there were peacocks, where the carpets, to which I was closer than to the ceiling, seemed as splendid as stories themselves, I was accommodated by intelligent adults, who accepted me as welcomingly as they did my father, who must often have been there on business.

National Trust houses began to be a positive pleasure, though it was not as such that I thought of them, when I was very young. The houses to which we went most often were Culzean, on the Ayrshire coast, and Brodick, on the Isle of Arran. I recall worrying my mother one day by saying to the old man who lived at The Hirsel that I preferred his dog to his house. The National Trust House I loved the most was Pitmedden, up in Aberdeenshire, although getting there involved a great deal of stopping to be sick. At Culzean there were ducks, Indian Runners and blotchy Muscovies, both species said by their curator to be good eaters, but nothing like as greedy as the swans, that would be content only with a 'jeely piece'. There was at Brodick a splendid porcelain and silver duck, perhaps Chinese, that was the first grotesque and thrilling artefact I was ever moved by. It says something for my father's nerve that he let me sit in a room alone with the fabulous thing, while he went up ladders and mixed size and paint.

He was reckless around buildings and that was another reason I resented them. He would climb anywhere, along anything, over rot and glass and splintering wood, to get to whatever it was he wanted to see – or to nothing at all. I was convinced he would fall, and I would shriek, which must have caused him almost to fall more than once. Like many people who are not strong, he was pigheaded, and practical with it. All my life I was convinced he'd die because of buildings, and when he did die, mixed with the other emotions, I felt a small re-lief; at least now he couldn't fall off a ladder tracking down some infinitesimal architectural detail. At Culzean he seemed to hang in the rotunda and I stared up. He was, those of you who did not know him will have gathered, very patient. Later, at Bute House, I think, he painted trompe l'oeil Thorvaldsen lozenges on a ceiling, difficult work involving subtle use of shading and a spectrum of different whites. I read him *A Hundred and One Dalmatians* for inspiration.

There were sudden worries for me, after my father got a car – it went, I think, with the job at the National Trust – because he was a passionate trespasser all his life. I wish some-one had told me then that, as I now believe, there isn't, or is not quite yet, perhaps I should say, any law of trespass in Scotland. I would imagine my mild but relentlessly curious father in prison each time we opened a gate blazoned with prohibitions, pushed up the choked drive, and walked up to, and sometimes into, and always around, some neglected beauty. Now, I look at the catalogue of Roy Strong, Marcus Binney and John Harris's exhibition *The Destruction of the Country House* and I understand more of what was in my father's mind. Mavis-bank, where my half brother and sister I gather acted as guard dogs overnight on occasion, was the house we went to again and again, and the Pineapple, now rescued by John Smith, who gave this lecture two years ago, and his Landmark Trust.

One of the last houses where we trespassed together was in Hampshire; the Grange, near Basingstoke. It was the most vastly monumental neo-classical house, owned at that time by the Ministry of Defence, who had just bought it from the Baring family. Unlike Scotland, the Ministry of Defence is unenlightened and does have a law of trespass. Their seriousness was reinforced by notices announcing the presence of killer dogs, razor wire, and, very possibly, marksmen. The Grange lies just above its own long lake in a deep green English valley. Someone had blown the constituent parts of the house up in the air and they had landed so far from one another that the cupola that had sat atop the house now seemed a distant summer-house, until you looked more closely. We were accompanied by some friends of mine, a couple, she pregnant and he a nervous wreck; also by my elder son, who could just crawl. What remained of The Grange was stone and untrustworthy beams. The Ministry of Defence had failed to observe the first law of security; they had not hidden their ladders under lock and key. I tried to distract my father, but it was too late. He was off. The ladders were of the narrow springy sort used, it seemed to me, in the Big Top.

I kept look out for the killer dogs. Daddy left the ladder and started his tightrope walk among the beams behind the great house's mighty operatic portico. My nervous friend suddenly swarmed up the ladder and was gone, showing no trace of nerves. His pregnant wife followed. I held to the ground, the baby my excuse. If I had not had him, I am sure even

I, timid and with no sense of balance, would have followed my father. He had the way of inspiring others and of encouraging them without nagging them. He was both direct and subtle, another characteristic of those who are best at communicating their enthusiasms. His effect upon these – quite unarchitecturally-literate – friends was to make them follow him like the Pied Piper.

When he came down from the ruined innards of The Grange, it was by another route, down a fall of rubble and nettles at the back of the house. Surveying the chaos of stone and mangled detail, punctuated with aggressive governmental ordinances, he said that he didn't understand why I didn't go there regularly to picnic.

Now you can't get anywhere near Northington Grange, there really are guard dogs at the entrance of the drive. The whole place has evidently been rebuilt to the specifications required by the hospitality rules of the MoD, and there are dark and possibly misleading rumours about the transactions conducted there. I feel fortunate to have seen the house before it had been wholly removed from itself, when its beauty and grandeur were still to be caught. In this hall tonight and in many other places there must be people who owe their first enthusiasm about houses, streets or towns to such outings with my father.

Again with offspring, this time two of them, we went to look at a house of leisurely open-faced handsomeness. It had been the house of dukes and was now a hotel, with competing wallpapers and a deep freeze in the front hall, where the proprietor and his wife were having an exhaustive argument. It was about the display of food for a wedding buffet that was due to start within the hour. It was a meal generously and bafflingly composed; mainly chipolatas and Russian salad, but also a lot of wafers.

Here I must interrupt to say that but for a few cigarettes and a Crunchie bar this could easily have been an ideal meal in my father's book. He was the least greedy of men and his tastes had been formed by rationing. Peaches that had not seen the inside of a tin were to him bitter fruit.

The hall of this fine, neglected house, had been weirdly partitioned with hardboard, some of it decorated with that architectural detailing in easily broken hard plastic that you can buy in DIY shops. In this case ceiling roses were applied to vertical partitions, giving a drunken and tribal effect whose scale was anyway much smaller than that of the original proportions and their mouldings. On the stairs blazed a Super Ser Calorgas heater. It made no difference. Strikingly, there were Christmas decorations up for the wedding. It was late summer. The house was freezing with damp.

Little could be more annoying for the busy and already strained proprietor of an hotel, preparing for the arrival of many guests, than to be approached by a very polite but entirely stubborn lunatic – and some of the lunatic's descendants – keen to investigate the covings of his establishment. The hotelier and his wife were furious, he in Greek/Scots and she in pure Scots.

After ten minutes, however, my father was laying out plates and advising on table layout, tweaking poinsettias and re-curling crepe paper streamers and tissue paper bells. Because he gave people time, he seemed to iron the panic out of them. We looked all over the fire-door-beleaguered house while the actual wedding party took place. Only with the greatest reluctance would the hotelier part with my father.

Which brings me to the business of talking to strangers. No one who knew my father well can have missed out on the frustrating sequence of events that went as follows: make an arrangement to meet – always too infrequent an event; meet, in some favoured ruin or pub, or both; spend the whole encounter watching spellbound while Colin made fast friends with the only other human for a ten mile radius, or the tramp at the door of the pub. At Rycote Abbey in Oxfordshire, my husband and I watched entranced and tense as my father listened to the story of the lonely lady from National Monuments in the rain. The rain didn't bother him a bit, but nor did the aeroplane he had to catch. Another time, we were being taken round Mellerstain with a group of Americans from the Buccleugh Studies Course. My father was 'doing' the tour. A human being innocent of snobbery, as I've said, and not interested in personages, he was the perfect companion with whom to see a building. His Buccleugh Studies ladies clearly enjoyed themselves, though I think they were surprised to be told nothing in the way of gossip, no family titbits, or anecdotal icing on the – already rich – architectural cake. One lady wanted something a bit more personal and went in detail into the colours she would have used to decorate it had Mellerstain been her house. It was a slow tour. My father didn't just hear her out; he was interested, went into how her plans might be realised, and so on. There is a short story by the contemporary writer Adam Mars-Jones in which the narrator wonders elegiacally of a dead man how much time he had wasted in his life writing the word 'only' after the sum on his cheques, in an act of somehow un-necessary, but elegant, defiance. My father's life was full of such acts, troubles taken, talent freely given. I don't suppose he behaved in this way consciously; it was his demeanour, and he would never have considered time spent in this way wasted. He had two small ways of wasting time as far as I know: going out to post a letter and humming. Towards the end of his life he was working so hard and sleeping so little, although he still remained misleadingly young-looking, that he fell asleep at table sometimes, waking up with a startled green glare.

Although it should not, perhaps, be so, it seems often to be the case that artists with an understanding of landscape or of architectural form are less happy with the human per-spective. Think of the transparent figures in Claude, the irrelevant homuncular cut-outs in the shadows of Piranesi. In these works it might be argued that the irrelevance of the human is itself irrelevant; they are works of myth and psychology, and eventually human in the grandest sense since they were made by sublimely gifted humans. Yet most of us have to live on the human scale while also being shown glimpses of the greater plan. My father under-stood this intimately. He wrote about statues in towns, calling them 'Permanent People':

> If the classical system is effectively an extension of human scale, a more literal
> one is provided by the town's statues. To put up one of these, unless one is

simply adding to a perfunctory line-up of notabilities like that of the Pincio gardens in Rome, is to undertake a major commitment in townscape. Its subject may well have been a living character in the town and as such he will have been related to it like anyone else, but the relationship is now to be permanent and formal. Whatever can be conveyed of his personality or attributes (Sir Walter Scott's dog, William Pitt's nose) must be subsidiary and if possible relevant to the statue's main job, which is to inhabit and demonstrate a town space. In Edinburgh three very diverse figures perform this role at the three successive junctions of George Street with its cross-streets; the histrionic King George IV, the suavely rhetorical Prime Minister, Pitt, the convinced, expository cleric Thomas Chalmers. Always concerned with space, when statues stand before a building they look away from it; thus the Duke of Wellington, conscious of form as always, leads the charge from the door of Register House on his prancing war horse, right across the already powerful axis of Waterloo Place and over the bridge to Edinburgh's Old Town. In Glasgow, leaving heroics to the mighty portico of Stirling's library, he sits more ceremonially and on a quieter mount to look down Ingram Street. Not all Glasgow's statues are so well sited, some of them having been displaced by traffic. The magnificent early eighteenth-century equestrian bronze of William III which used to dignify the line of Trongate has been unhappily penned in a small fenced-in plot near the Cathedral. As real as people (in some respects more so) and substantial as buildings, statues form a link between the two; a link also in time, for they are witnesses not only of times past but of times passing, as sundials through bright days, bird-perches always, sadly dripping in the rain, snow-hatted in winter.

It is a typically witty piece of writing, veering towards anthropomorphism without losing its seriousness. One of the dullest days I spent with my father (almost a contradiction in terms) was when East Kilbride was going up. He went over to make a drawing of it to go with something he had written, I think for the *Scotsman*. He never wrote about a building or drew it without actually seeing it. That is considerably rarer than it sounds. We stood in East Kilbride. The weather was yet again wet. But we did not leave until my father got East Kilbride down on paper, and got it right. A reiterated and high regard for that town, indeed, may be found in his large output of architectural articles for the *Scotsman*. At one point he declares that it is where he would live, were that not the New Town of Edinburgh. Irvine and mighty, Egyptian, Cairness, high in Aberdeenshire, seem to have been his other choices. As I've said he did not see or hear received opinions. This left him without cynicism and clear-eyed. The only area where he was predictable was in his lifelong shrinking from what one might characterise as fat-catness. Around smugness and overcomfort he was miserable. He had very few material wants, though he liked light-fittings and was fond of almost anything from an ironmonger's. I suppose he was an anarcho-pacifist Fabian in his politics, or at least his temperament, though his childhood as a chorister and child of an unusually devout and musical mother had instilled in him an attachment to the liturgy, if not to the liturgical.

Rather as with the weekend visits to the National Galleries of Scotland that I sometimes resented at the time, the churchgoing that only desisted when I was quite old – about twelve – is now one of the things for which I am most grateful to my father.

It is the same with the paintings in the great National Galleries here. They were of course hung very differently then, the modern ones even in a different place, but those paintings became for an only child, which is what I was at first, almost like family, if it is possible to envisage the family in which belong both Rubens's repulsively gourmandising Herodias and Velasquez's old woman cooking eggs. The fine twist of rose in the paint at the end of the nose of Tiepolo's Pharaoh's daughter, and the absorbed quiet of Matisse's little girl painting, the peculiar Araldite murkiness of the Ben Nicholsons combined with their spatial radiance, all these extraordinary things became familiar. Pictures and buildings were not ever for me things to be talked about self-consciously or in a spirit of artiness, with bated breath. They were things we lived among. No sense of ownership came into it, any more – or less – than a sense of ownership afflicts the person walking down a street in his home town. What a luxury this was.

My father's own visual education seems to have begun early. His own father drew and was a friend of artists. He had aunts who drew and painted. His napkin ring, on which his name is engraved in the hand of his father, who fought in both World Wars and was killed in the Second, reveals a linear heredity. The writing is similar to my father's hand; it is the hand of an artist; regular, elegant and legible, without unnecessary flourishes. McWilliams have been doctors and sailors, sometimes both together. They are mathematical and musical, often again the both together, as is the way with these two arts.

Early on, my father took to drawing in pen and ink and in pencil. Often, he illustrated his correspondence, with a line that, as it grew more certain, became ever more truthful and funnier. He admired the caricatures of houses so brilliantly conjured by Osbert Lancaster in *Homes Sweet Homes*, and could himself caricature as well as make portraits of buildings, people and cats. Sometimes his line is like that of Ronald Searle. As a rule, it is more anchored, less filigreed; although his drawings are fanciful, they are disciplined. He excelled at that demanding craft, decorative drawing, which can so easily become sugary or loose. The gaunt 1950s' line came naturally to him. His drawing master at Charterhouse was a Czech, whom he admired and spoke of all his life.

Certainly he preferred Cambridge to Charterhouse, where, he always told me, he worked for alternate terms and took a terrible scunner to William Rees-Mogg. He liked Jim Prior and Simon Raven, two very different men. Asked what he remembered of my father, Simon Raven said that he recalled his eyes.

At Cambridge, he moved from Classics to Architecture, and was happier. I thought that at this point you might like to stop listening to me.

And listen instead to this tape recording of a record made of my father and other undergraduates celebrating the sixth centenary of the College in Caius Court on the stroke of 10 p.m. on 17 June 1948.

People very often happen upon their great love by sidewise route, and it was so with my father. I do not think he envisaged his life remaining for its duration in this country when first he came up here. He was satirical about some fancy Edinburgh ways, just as he was sometimes a touch snippy, although my stepmother is Dutch, about certain Dutch delicacies – raw herring, hot oily cakes or *oliebalen* – although towards the end of his life he wrote saying to me that he was beginning to find Dutch art as rewarding and moving as that of Italy, his first artistic and architectural love. The trips they made to Holland were a continual source of contemplation to him; he came to admire the courage of a nation holding off the sea and presenting so calm a face to the world in its art.

When I was a child, this city was being knocked about, stripped back and gutted. You will know better than I how this process is not at an end even now. 'Process' is the wrong word, implying as it does some natural cycle. Many demolitions took place, sometimes in the greatest good faith, sometimes for reasons that bear no looking into. Many cities, of course, fared worse than this one. Nonetheless, it was a city so remarkable that it behoved it to be treated as a special case. Long before the preservation and conservation of buildings were – as they are now in the case of certain 'high profile' buildings – causes that were dear to the public heart, my father and like-minded people saw what may now seem to us an obvious link: that between humans and where they live and what they see. Some of my earliest memories of my father are of the protests he organised in attempting to forestall the demolition of buildings. He was an almost pathologically unostentatious person, as you will have gathered, but he was not embarrassed by his own unconventionality either. So that when he threatened to lie in the path of a bulldozer in his – shamefully overruled – fight to save the old New Club, he was sincere. He may even have done it. In the way a daughter will mythologise her father, I believe that he did. In our house, there were continual campaigns for buildings. In this way the buildings came to resemble failing, beloved, relatives, who must be brought back to rude health. Often as not, as many of you will know, they were euthanased in the dead of night. A scandal. A couple of years ago I was up here and was driven in from Turnhouse by a driver with a compendious knowledge of the city. He drove by an esoteric route. Only the grossest cynic would have said this might be to jack up the fare.

'How do you know all this?' I asked him. I was fearing his answer might be that he was an out-of-work architect.

'My family's big in demolition,' he said, 'but there's less of it to go round than there was, so I'm doing this.'

He was like a gamekeeper, passionately knowledgeable about what he destroyed . His enthusiasm for the buildings and – quite explicitly – for the principles behind the buildings of the New Town was a characteristic that is not unusual at all for the inhabitants of this city. How appalling that this relationship between a hive and its workers is not any longer practicable in many of the gutted cities of Britain, and hardly conceivable in the savaged metropolis of London.

My father's feeling for London was intense throughout his life. Quite shortly before he died, he took a bus trip to Sydenham, where he was born, with his younger brother Clement. They sat up in the brow of the bus, and were very excited. It is a charming picture. The attachment to non-monumental parts of monumental towns was as deep in him as the talking to strangers. I have a suspicion that it was his particular pleasure in London to find the smallest and if possible nastiest places to eat on his trips there, usually to pursue business and take in a, preferably very long, preferably baroque, opera. Sometimes fate tricked him and the restaurant would be good.

To return from London to Scotland, which became over the years not just his home but the object of his energies. Like many people who are chronically unwell, he had prodigious energy. His conviction grew that architectural conservation should be an obligatory part of the training of the future's architects which it is not, yet. He battled to get it onto the RIAS and RIBA compulsory requirements for training. He was in a good position, at a good time, and in a good place, to see the baneful consequences of ignoring the plain lessons of the past. He had been young and idealistic at the pitch of the architectural rape of the country in the nineteen sixties. The changes of the nineteen seventies in a society less authoritarian and polite than that of his youth did nothing to advance his frail faith in the common-sense of people with power and influence. His involvement with the Scottish Georgian Society and other organisations at every level shows, however, that he was far from disillusioned with the effectiveness of groups to preserve and conserve buildings. He saw the mess made by unfunnelled affluence in the 1980s, the fearful mirror glass and texmex lego malls rising even in this protected city. Of course, he also saw many good things. Many of you must be wondering as I am what he would have made of the new Opera House here, or the smartened up Morrison and Gibb building, now Standard Life, that stands at the end of the street where he lived from 1954–89, Warriston Crescent. I wonder, indeed, what he'd've made of the newly-opened opera house at Wick in Caithness, designed by that David Bryce earlier so vilified by Scott-Moncrieff. There are a thousand reasons for missing him; one of the greatest is not being able to see as well as I could when he was here.

The architecture of this country is so well worth seeing, as none of you here will need to be told. This is a small country with a multiplicity of styles, a strong tradition for public and private architecture, an extraordinarily laminated history, close aesthetic relations with continental Europe through its history, deep roots in the architecture of distant lands like Russia and India, to which we sent our engineers. An English friend said to me, 'All Scots architecture is pastiche.' There's someone who can't take a joke, especially not if it's set in stone. I refer that person, any other doubters too, to the great, and growing, *catalogue raisonée*, of Scottish buildings, the *Buildings of Scotland*. The hardest thing to write is, perhaps, a great poem or a great reference book. To last and to succeed the reference book should have something of the great poem to it. Pick up a volume of that series and you will hear through the gazetting of architectural detail the old, various, voices of this country.

One of the reasons we need to understand architecture is that it explains to us something of the time that came before us. I wouldn't go so far in this country, that has conspicuously made them work, as to say that New Towns were a contradiction in terms – after all, we're in one now – but it is hard for us to live without history, just as it is hard for a child to flourish alone. It does not know who to be. My father addresses the question of the town and time again and again in his work. It was, after all, in its practical application, conservation, his great subject, and the practical one we can help to carry on for him.

Since I have been speaking so personally, I hope you will forgive me if I finish up by talking about a novel of my own, called *Debatable Land*. It's dedicated to my father, who died when I was quite far into it. His death torpedoed that version to bits. It had been a linear story of one man's growing up, a *Bildungsroman*; as far from autobiography as could be, except that the hero was from Edinburgh, the son of a fishmonger and a fishgutter, both from Leith. Novelists are always asked if they are writing about themselves. It's the only question that one is asked more frequently than 'Can you get me on telly?' No, I don't write about myself, but the characters I imagined in this book share many of my feelings about Edinburgh.

I'd no idea what my novel was going to do. It expired when my father expired. I spent some time trying to bring it round, but it was gone. Stevenson had been much in my mind, and the past, that comes to get you when a parent goes. Much as one sees slides, I saw repeated visions of this city, laid out to view in a bowl. It came to me that this bowl was the bowl at the old Camera Obscura. I put the book in the hands of the city, together with the other ideas that had been preoccupying me, especially the tension between the ideas of north and south, and the notion I had had all along of setting Scotland up against the South Seas. I wanted to write a novel about the sea, because a boat is a pleasingly tense place where a lot goes on even when nothing is apparently happening. And I fancied an adventure story because people behave like themselves when they are scared. All these things came together in a form that I wanted to be slippery, as it were, as life is, with things so interfused as to be inextricable, the funny with the sad, the land with the sea. People are contrary, I think, so I had my characters journey to the south of the world in order to find that they had brought with them what they loved, even though they thought they were escaping it. For the three central characters of the book what they find at the back end of the world is their country, Scotland – and family love. Actually, in a way I think my father wrote parts of this book. Here's a bit about the Camera Obscura.

> In the dark they stood around a low white bowl, about a yard wide, while a tubby man, dressed in the civvy uniform of a commissionaire, tried to get the measure of them, like someone shaking a bag of sugar for lumps.
>
> 'Here in this room you will see your own home town, brought by a periscope and mirrors down into this white dish. I shall indicate the places I mention with the baton I hold here in my hand.' He tapped the white stick thrice in the bowl, into which light at once fell from a tight point above it so that the children stood about an inverted cone of light. The light was not

electric or warm. It was the light of day. It seemed refreshing in that room that smelt of serge and boys.

'Very well. The mirrors, Ian, please.' A cranking sound came from a corner. A small man in the brown overall ironmongers wore at that time looked up with the furtively busy movement of a rodent. He was turning a handle whose noise described its effect, the circular motion pressing up into, disengaging and raising metal bars attached to plates that moved with a squeaking sigh and a more precarious, delicate sound, like teeth in one's own head.

'Thank you, Ian. That'll be the mirrors marrying now. Tighten up there, Ian, till I see it clear. There we are. The city of Edinburgh, boys, laid out in a bowl.'

Not the whole city at once, but parts of it in turn spilt down by the mirrors into the bowl, a tour the boys could not have accomplished on their inattentive feet. The colours were the same as when the boys had left the world outside of the Camera Obscura. The quality of high brightness they had was on account of the darkness from which the eye looked. There was no impression of the idealised colour of film, its incipient sunsetty glow. The colours were true to the tabby, pewter, lilac and soot of the slate and smoke of the city.

'One mile in length runs Princes Street whose stores are used by the highest in the land. Over here the North British Hotel, whose clock you will observe is a punctual five minutes fast. Passengers at Waverley Station therefore,' he waved the baton, 'are less likely to miss their trains. The two great galleries of Scotland are here at the foot of the Mound, sorely in need of a clean as you will observe from the state of the Queen.' The baton flicked a youthful coal-black Queen Victoria seated on the roof of a low-columned building on whose black steps a man scraped at a fiddle. No noise, of course, came.

'The Scott Monument further down Princes Street is a memorial to a great son of Scotland the Laird of Abbotsford. You will see him at his books inside this,' he took a breath as though about to use a phrase from the French, 'highly ornamented example of the neo-Gothic.'

Ian turned his crank again and the sound came as a shock. It was peculiar to see the town alive but not to hear its life. As though taken over by the invasive silence to be found in involuntary church going, the children redoubled their silence, if you can double nothing.

Alec began to ache, not with boredom so much as concentration. The spin of the greasy iron sounded like the chain of a playground swing, slowed only just bearably. Alec was nervous in the comfortable way a beloved child of regular habits feels hunger. He was about to know how to allay what ailed him.

The man in his uniform began again. The decorations on his chest were slim bits of colour like a girl's dress caught in a door hinge each time he bent forward into the cone of light.

'Here of course we have Princes Street Gardens, open to all for recreation. The world-famous floral clock may be seen just here, giving the correct time in many colourful blooms, kept fresh by careful replanting. Only in the depth of winter does it rest. Are there any questions now?'

Since a couple were embracing next to the congested planting of the floral clock, one of the boys had to speak, to release the tension.

Heck asked, 'Is it the flowers keep the clock going or the other way about?' At that moment the door of a small house on a stick set behind the floral clock burst open and a stiff wooden bird was ejected. It bobbed three times. The sound it made, inaudible to the boys, apparently shocked the couple whose deep embrace they had been following in detail. The man had his hand behind the woman's head as though he was injecting her with his face. When the bird sprang out, they leapt apart as if they had just found out they had been making a mistake.

It was a surprise to Alec to see that neither of these people was distinguishable as a person who had recently been kissing. He thought it must show somehow.

'The gardeners keep the clock going. And here we have the Mound itself, aye, Ian, right you are, heated underground in winter, boys, as you may know, by a warm blanket lying just beneath the surface, recently installed at no small cost.' A maroon City of Edinburgh bus was straining like a beetle up the steep hill towards the Old Town, leaving the Castle off to its right. It was a cold mistless day with a hidden glare of sun that from time to time flashed off glass or metal as they made their cooped tour of an airy city into which they had never roamed so far, whose sea they saw at the one reach of their Olympian view, whose lion-shaped presiding hill, Arthur's Seat (Why is Holyrood? Because it looks up Arthur's Seat. Alec thought the riddle before he meant to, out of habit laid too long to wipe out), and dark crags at the other.

At some point during that afternoon a ladybird blundered on to the dish where the city displayed itself tantalisingly bowlful by bowlful. Alec realised that he had been walking about the streets with the same unaware confusion as the insect now showed, marching through and over people, houses, churches, gardens, schools, law courts, graveyards, libraries, as though only it was real and they were just light thrown by a mirror. It stood unaware among the thorny arms of the crown on top of the High Kirk of St Giles. It meandered down the wide, granite-laid streets of the New Town, before falling over the edge and out of his sight into the daytime darkness.

Most peculiar of all was the silence from these streets, whose surface was of setts, blocks of stone laid brickwise, a surface that, outside of the Camera Obscura, gave richness to the sound of vehicles and a stony literal accompaniment to the progress of people or horses.

Here was their city, voiceless, displayed. The silence kept Alec's attention and enclosed him. When Hector took out his kazoo and began to polish it on his backside, Alec was for a moment in terror of the noise he knew must come, as though he had made a decision for life to choose sight above hearing.

The ladybird is a posthumous present to my father, who used to describe the havoc wrought by a fly on a slide of the Venus de Milo when he was a young man.

The thread that connects these random memories of my father and makes them seem coherent to me is his character: witty, alert, energetic, ever sensible of irony yet full of innocent perseverance. I don't know if I have made it seem at all coherent to you. My father had too proper a sense of seriousness ever to be solemn, but, thinking about him now, I will risk just a very few solemn observations.

The title that I began with as little more than a decorative conceit, seems to me to hint at a serious truth about visual education, architecture, and their bearing on society. You can live with an I (capital 'I') in the sense of putting up with (or perhaps giving yourself over to) it; or you can live with an eye ('E.Y.E.') in the sense of being made more truly alive by it, but it is very hard to do both. The two things that strike me most about my father, the things that I have mainly been remembering today, are his modesty and the alert curiosity with which he looked at the world. A society that is visually alert must be built upon both these qualities. In order to look, we must be modest enough to believe that the world around us is intrinsically more interesting than our individual selves, and humble enough to put our-selves all our lives to school to try to understand the many visual languages that surround us with meaning. Those languages and those meanings have great physical powers of survival, but without education, which is only another way of saying intelligent, properly sceptical tradition, they can easily be lost for a generation or a whole age. Confident, democratic societies – fifth-century Athens, fifteenth-century Florence, seventeenth-century Holland, Georgian Edinburgh – have been permeated by this understanding. It provided them with much more than an aesthetic thrill: it helped to define their common sense, by constantly refining the delicate equation in any civilised society between individual and civic require-ments. Architecture is still by definition the most social of all the arts – the one which un-questionably has the greatest influence on the lives of most people and the one which draws together, and, as it were, houses all the other visual arts. We live, as Carlyle and Ruskin fore-saw with sobering accuracy well over a hundred years ago, in societies that are dedicated to mass production, and sometimes seem nearly strangled by its physical pressures. I find it difficult to be sure whether societies get the architects they deserve, or whether the process works the other way around. But being my father's daughter, I am quite sure that we more than ever need intelligent architects and conservation architects, (not merely preservation architects) to save us now.

It has been an honour to have been asked to speak to you here in this place, to which I first came to hear a lecture given by my father. On that occasion I'm sure I slept. I hope you haven't, or, if you have, that you have slept well.

I must thank everyone involved in arranging this lecture. I know my father was greatly honoured to be made an Honorary Fellow of the RIAS, and later an FRIAS. Thank you for giving me this opportunity of talking to you a little about the person whose work we are here to commemorate – and, thanks to many of you, to continue.

Book Reviews

Gavin Stamp and Sam McKinstry (eds), *Greek Thomson*, Edinburgh
University Press, 1994, Hardback, £25, ISBN 0 7486 0480 4.

The architecture of the Scottish architect Alexander 'Greek' Thomson is among the most
powerful and evocative of the nineteenth century. The gaunt triumvirate of churches, the
soot-blackened villas and terraces of houses and the nightmarish commercial chambers
which he designed in and around Glasgow are at once austere and eclectic, scholarly and
barbaric. They evoke, more than anything else, the apocalyptic visions of the painter John
Martin – 'buildings of the most powerful kind: vast cubic masses playing against each
other, interminable colonnades of some unacknowledged order, temples of inconceivable
solemnity and exotic style'.

This is not a biography of 'Greek' Thomson, but rather a collection of essays on aspects of
the work of this highly original architect, intended to be read in conjunction with Ronald
McFadzean's 'Life' of Thomson published in 1979. Introduced by an elegant reminiscence by
the late Sir John Summerson – his last work for publication – the book is divided into five
sections. These explore the background to Thomson's architecture; his theory and ideals; the
urbanism of his architecture; his interiors and the international ramifications of the architect's
work. Within this framework seventeen individual essays examine diverse subjects, among
them Thomson's literary and pictorial sources; contemporaneous developments in Scottish
architecture; his urban façades; his rare surviving furniture and interior decoration and the
influence on Thomson of the theologian Friedrich Schliermacher, the colourist Daniel
Cottier and the publications of the American designer Minard Lafever. The penultimate essay
compares the work of Thomson, Mackintosh and Frank Lloyd Wright and the volume is
concluded by Gavin Stamp's fine and passionately written tribute to the architect.

This welcome and interesting diversity casts a generous net over its subject. However, the
limited amount of biographical information on Thomson and the paucity of his surviving
writings makes it inevitable that the contributors have a tendency to repeat the information
available. Choice quotes from Thomson's 'Inquiry', a vitriolic attack on the Gothic style of
1866 and the precious Haldane Lectures of 1874 are regularly pressed into service to
illustrate particular points. How one wishes that more information had survived and that
Thomson's lost paper of 1853, tantalisingly entitled 'The Sources and Elements of Art
Considered in Connection with Architectural Design', would emerge! But there are many
revelations in the book and this is a collection of individual essays rather than a sustained
flight of literary endeavour.

The most serious and surprising omission is that the contributors make virtually no reference to the influence of Indian, and particularly Hindu, architecture on Thomson – an observation first made, I believe, by Sir Albert Richardson. Apart from Alexander Stoddart, who briefly notes in his essay on the architect's architectural sculpture, the Indian derivation of the elephant-atlantes in the South Kensington Museum design of 1864, and Stamp who, in his summing up, makes an interesting comparison with Lutyens' work in Imperial Delhi, none of the writers discuss the probabilities of Indian inspiration. Instead, they choose to concentrate on the architects' acknowledged debt to Egyptian, Greek and Assyrian architecture and his known admiration of the visions of John Martin. However, what is overlooked is that much of Thomson's architectural vocabulary can be found in the architecture of India. A glance through the views of Indian buildings by Thomas and William Daniell, reproduced in aquatint form in the six volumes of 'Oriental Scenery' between 1795–1808, reveal many possible sources. The sugarloaf tower of the Queen's Park Church and the elongated domed cupola of the church tower on St Vincent Street are startingly reminiscent of the forms found in Daniell's views – particularly the Hindu temples at Agori in Uttar Pradesh and of the Sun Temple at Deo in Bihar. The banded ashlar on the flanks of the Caledonia Road Church may also derive from the strips of masonry which articulate the steep sides of these temples. Even the overladen, 'Martinian' quality of Thomson's architecture can be detected in Daniell's view of the great temple at Srivilliputtar near Madras. Other Thomsonian tricks; the trabeated loggias with projecting eaves, the squat, highly decorated columns and the relentless horizontal emphasis which governs his work may be of 'Hindoostani' inspiration. Thomson's possible appropriation of Indian features, robed in Grecian disguise, is all the more intriguing given the undoubted Hellenic influences on the art and architecture of the subcontinent.

The book is well illustrated with photographs of Thomson's work, including many melancholy archive photographs of buildings now demolished. It is sobering to reflect how much of Thomson's work has been destroyed in comparatively recent years. These images, together with reproductions of the original architect's drawings, source and comparative material and the line drawings of many of his buildings will be of real value to those with a serious interest in Thomson's architecture. Likewise, the select bibliography on Thomson at the end of the volume which wisely eschews the 'mass of poorly researched material displaying a remarkable misunderstanding of his achievement'.

For all his innovation my overriding impression is that Thomson is a curiously retardetaire architect for his time – a brilliant maverick, strangely isolated and out of place by 1875, the year of his death. Unlike Mackintosh, whose work appeared excitingly modern in his own time, Thomson's architecture had more in common with the work of men like Goodridge or Donthorn – Regency-eclectic survivors – than the architectural champions of the Goth-ridden age in which he died. To me this is demonstrated by Andrew McMillan's essay which points out, in a rather different context, that Holmwood, the luxurious 'Grecian' villa

Thomson built in 1857 was completed only two years before the Red House of William Morris and Philip Webb. Let us hope that these contradictory and 'difficult' aspects of 'Greek' Thomson's work will serve, as Stamp expresses the wish, to 'spare him the dreadful fate of becoming an object of selective and uncritical adulation – such as perverts our understanding of Mackintosh's genius'.

Tim Knox

Karen Moon, *George Walton Designer and Architect*, White Cockade
Publishing, Oxford, 1993, Hardback, £30, ISBN 1 873487 01 0.

The author begins: 'I first met George Walton's son, Edward, in 1979. Conversations with
Edward were always stimulating and enlightening. Though his father died when he was still
a child, Edward retained a deep respect and admiration for him, and held an excellent archive
of his work; from time to time, he would dig amongst his treasures and bring out some jewel
to show me.' Two memoirs are included by Edward and Walton's grandson, George Walton
Scott, which create a vivid introduction to the man and an insight into his personality, broad
interests and methods of working.

Walton's life is traced from its beginnings in Glasgow, where he was born in 1867, the
youngest in a large family of whom five were gifted artists. George attended art classes at
the School of Art, where Fra Newbury had arrived as principal in 1885, keen to stimulate
the decorative arts. Through his brother and sisters, Edward Arthur, Helen, Connie and
Hannah, he had the opportunity to mix with a wide cross-section of the contemporary local
artistic society, women artists, the Glasgow Boys and members of the School of Art.
Employed at the British Linen Bank from the age of thirteen, it was the artistic activities of
his family which really interested him. Influences from England, particularly Whistler's
innovative exhibition interiors and Aesthetic Movement furniture, combined with the
emphasis in Glasgow on the decorative, were undoubtedly important stimuli to Walton's
ambition to form a decorating company.

The 1888 Glasgow International Exhibition provided a boost for many commercial
operations and artists in the city. Walton received a commission from Kate Cranston to
redecorate her Argyle Street tearoom. He left the bank and opened his own showroom,
George Walton & Co., Ecclesiastical and House Decorations. By 1891 the company was flourish-
ing. Imitating the craft workshop ideal of Morris, the production of stained glass and stencil-
ling, furniture, fireplaces, carpets, fabrics, cutlery and glassware was added to the initial
activities of painting and paperhanging. Walton designed for his clients progressive interiors.
Catering for individual customers' needs, he provided rooms which were both comfortable
and pleasurable to live in.

The company was a formative influence on the Glasgow Style and became known to a
wider audience through more public commissions. Miss Cranston's new lunch and tea rooms
in Buchanan Street, and the Rowntree cafés in Scarborough, provided the opportunity to
create unified decorative schemes, which were a huge success.

Moving to London in 1897, his artistic exhibition designs for the progressive photographic
group 'The Linked Ring' were a complete innovation. Exhibition work and shop designs,
in the Glasgow Style, for Kodak shops in London and on the continent gained wide publicity
... the catchword was 'Kodakoration, the decorative work of George Walton'.

Walton turned to architecture quite naturally; his work in shop design had provided direct
architectural experience. At The Leys, built in 1901, he combined his love of classical

symmetry with the picturesque manner of Voysey, using Arts and Crafts vernacular materials. Architecture was his ambition. It enabled him not only to control the interior, where he harmonised all the elements to the last detail, but also to integrate the decorative work fully with the building.

His versatility in designing quite contrasting structures, suitable for a specific location or function is illustrated by his work for James Davison. Wern Fawr, a fortress site built in roughly cut Cambrian stone contrasts with The White House, Davison's riverside home at Shiplake, open to the garden and light, a house for summer living. The quirky Log Cabin houseboat, complete with American Indian motifs, can be compared to his last work, in memory of his patron, the simple Chapel of St George, Cap d'Antibes.

The furniture designs in Walton's design ledger and some additional drawings originally from this ledger in the George Walton Archive show him to have been one of the leading furniture designers of the period. He assimilated ideas from sources as diverse as Mackmurdo and Sheraton, producing designs which demonstrate his complete understanding of the materials and techniques of construction.

Illustrated with 233 plates of which 33 are in colour, the book provides a rich secondary source for reference. Sources are given for illustrations but an index to the plates with notes, to parallel the detailed footnotes, would have been most useful.

Publication of the book coincided with an exhibition organised by Glasgow Museums and subsequently shown at Brighton Museum and Art Gallery. It is very readable and presents a complete picture of Walton's achievement and a sense of his place within contemporary art and architecture movements, both in Glasgow and in a wider context. The commissions are meticulously documented and illustrated, providing a logically organised body of detailed material for analysis. The evidence that the author presents so eloquently leaves the reader in no doubt as to Walton's primary position as designer and architect.

Elizabeth Hancock
Keeper of Collections, Hamilton Museum

Miles Glendinning and Stefan Muthesius, *Tower Block: Modern Public Housing in England, Scotland, Wales and Northern Ireland*, Yale University Press, 1994, Hardback, £40, ISBN 0 300 05444 0.

Fifty years since the end of the Second World War have seen a transformation of our urban landscape. This book records the literal rise of perhaps the most important single agent of that transformation; government promoted public housing in the United Kingdom.

The book is divided into three sections: 'Design', 'Production' and 'Breakdown', the last covering the simultaneous rejections, in the last twenty years of modern design and of the principles of social housing.

Of course public provision of housing did not begin in 1945. In their introduction the authors briefly discuss the development of the public sector from its foundation in 1919 in the face of post-war housing shortage and in consequence of the collapse of the private building of housing for rent in the years preceding the First World War. The authors demonstrate how interaction between central government and British municipalities transformed the urban scene, and they upset many accepted explanations on the way.

During the war an influential housing reform movement was active; publications on planning and rebuilding abounded, directed at a popular audience. The housing reformers' message opens *Tower Block*:

> The homes of the postwar years were to be homes of a new kind ... The postwar Modern dwelling had to be, and look, radically different, inside and out. For many, 'Modern' meant a new type of dwelling altogether, making use of completely new methods of construction. There was a host of new fittings; above all large windows, a separate bathroom and a kitchen with built-in cupboards, electric sockets in all the bedrooms and more. (p. 9)

So *Section I: Design*, begins by considering new and systematic theory, often influenced by continental sources: Frankfurt, the Bauhaus and Le Corbusier, including the message that high flats, properly planned, could actually enhance open space and daylight standards. Also there was a systematic social brief, ranging from the idea of community, to detailed specification of dwelling sizes to fit household need.

Technical and social theories did not lead inevitably to high flats as a general housing solution; the favoured pattern of the first post-war decade was 'mixed development', where flats were built alongside terraced houses. Nevertheless, many housing professionals and politicians were sold on flats, and large schemes of the 1940s and 1950s consisted entirely of flats in blocks of five storeys or more.

Thus far the arguments for high flats seem to be purely practical, but at the same time architects and planners were discussing the aesthetic values of tall buildings in urban design. Swedish social housing, and its characteristic form of slender tower or 'point' blocks set in landscaped surroundings, was generally admired, and from 1950 high flats were incorporated in mixed development avowedly to enhance the urban scene.

The second section of *Tower Block*, housing production, forms the meat of the book: from national and local policy documents, and interviews with politicians, officials and contractors involved in the great housing drive of the 1950s and 1960s, a complex but compelling account has been assembled, recording extremes of political idealism and industrial opportunism. Importantly, the skeins of politics and policy in London, in English regional areas, in Scotland and Northern Ireland, are separated and explained. It is for this that the interested reader must get hold of the book, to read and understand.

The authors show how the multi-storey block, developed primarily to secure sufficient housing in the face of land shortage, then applied as an element in urban design, was exploited to achieve sheer production. They also oppose the contention of other recent historians, that high flats were imposed on local councils by a conspiracy of government departments and the building industry (a plea that has been echoed by local authorities themselves).

The 'planners' threat, supported and impelled by government was to disperse population from the major conurbations by planned overspill, but as detailed discussion of Glasgow's housing drive shows, conflict was not simply between city and central government. While the city planning department sought to support the official line of dispersing population to new and expanded towns, housing divisions in the Scottish Office, also production oriented, formed a covert alliance with the Glasgow 'housers'. That support was the fruit of Glasgow's success, in the massive housing drive organised by Housing Convenor David Gibson, and the engineer Lewis Cross, in charge of sites and contracts. Thus Glasgow's housing revolution in the 1960s was locally propelled, 'resulting in blocks of an unfettered monumentality, unparalled at that date not only in these islands, but in Europe as a whole.'

Of course the real heroes were in Scotland, and the chapter on 'Scotland's housing Blitzkreig' is pivotal. Glasgow's achievements and example are central here, and the methods and successes of Gibson and Cross, the exploitation of every gap-site, development of peripheral and redevelopment sites to the highest possible density, repeated package-deal contracts awarded to reliable contractors, came to be admired and emulated throughout central Scotland.

Dick Mabon's national housing drive had no real counterpart in England and Wales, where initiative remained largely with individual local authorities, some of the most active of which are treated in this book. In Northern Ireland housing was eventually tackled by direct government intervention: quite another story. But in Scotland Gibson's legacy was secure; the cities, the county councils and burghs large and small were imbued with a crusading housing spirit, most of them seeking to acquire their 'multis', symbols of housing action and civic pride, reviving, as our authors say, the national tradition of monumental flat-building.

In the late 1960s and 1970s, widespread enthusiasm for high flats gave way to widespread hatred of them. That experience is still so close, and opinions still so strongly held, that I forbear to comment on the authors' views. I hope, though, that the reader will reach the final chapters informed by Muthesius and Glendinning's account of how we acquired the tower block legacy, and reflect upon their conclusions.

This remarkable book sets new standards in administrative and planning history, in the breadth of its field, its detail, and the clarity of its argument. Anyone concerned with housing and the urban environment must benefit from reading it. *Tower Block* is at the same time, a unique source of reference. Besides numerous photographs of the actors in the production story, often intimate and revealing, illustrations of the products, assembled from local councils, press, and contractors form a valuable design record. And to round off the work there is a gazetteer, listing all multi-storey developments by public housing authorities since 1945 (every one visited by the authors!), and a parallel index of journal references.

The high-rise era had its failures, some honestly recorded here, but in many high-rise schemes, where careful management and allocation policies have been maintained, there are waiting lists for vacancies. Increasingly housing professionals and tenants see these buildings as a resource to be valued and properly used.

In 1968 Professor Barry Cullingworth pointed out that if we suppose a house to last, on average, 100 years we should be replacing our housing stock at a 1% rate every year, for ever. Such a replacement rate has hardly ever been achieved anywhere; one exception was in Glasgow in those few years in the 1960s. Houses standing now must have a life expectancy of over 1,000 years at present rates, and that's a long time even for tenements. As sure as night follows day housing crisis will hit us again, and again the call will be for production. Will we learn from the high-rise experience, or just hope for better luck next time?

David Whitham